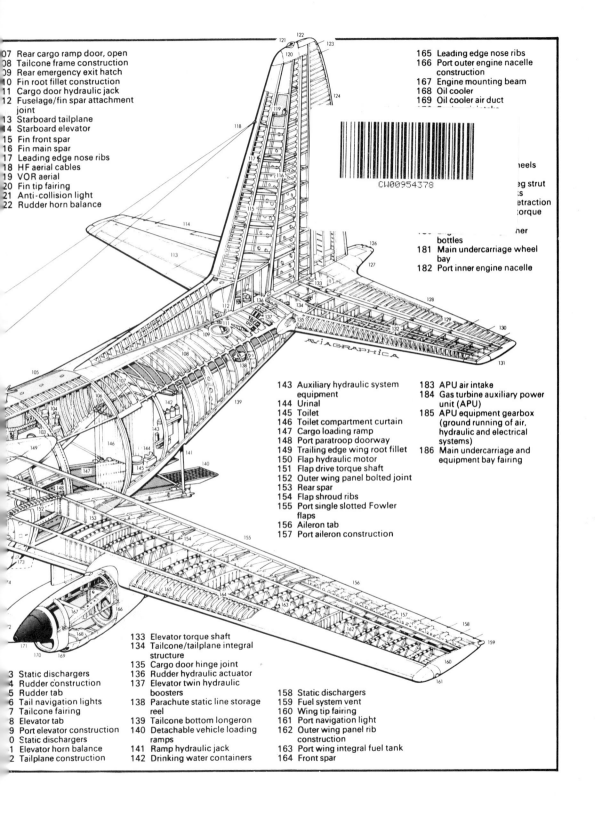

07 Rear cargo ramp door, open
08 Tailcone frame construction
09 Rear emergency exit hatch
10 Fin root fillet construction
11 Cargo door hydraulic jack
12 Fuselage/fin spar attachment joint
13 Starboard tailplane
14 Starboard elevator
15 Fin front spar
16 Fin main spar
17 Leading edge nose ribs
18 HF aerial cables
19 VOR aerial
20 Fin tip fairing
21 Anti-collision light
22 Rudder horn balance

165 Leading edge nose ribs
166 Port outer engine nacelle construction
167 Engine mounting beam
168 Oil cooler
169 Oil cooler air duct

...eels
...eg strut
...s
...etraction
...orque

...ner
bottles
181 Main undercarriage wheel bay
182 Port inner engine nacelle

143 Auxiliary hydraulic system equipment
144 Urinal
145 Toilet
146 Toilet compartment curtain
147 Cargo loading ramp
148 Port paratroop doorway
149 Trailing edge wing root fillet
150 Flap hydraulic motor
151 Flap drive torque shaft
152 Outer wing panel bolted joint
153 Rear spar
154 Flap shroud ribs
155 Port single slotted Fowler flaps
156 Aileron tab
157 Port aileron construction

183 APU air intake
184 Gas turbine auxiliary power unit (APU)
185 APU equipment gearbox (ground running of air, hydraulic and electrical systems)
186 Main undercarriage and equipment bay fairing

133 Elevator torque shaft
134 Tailcone/tailplane integral structure
135 Cargo door hinge joint
136 Rudder hydraulic actuator
137 Elevator twin hydraulic boosters
138 Parachute static line storage reel
139 Tailcone bottom longeron
140 Detachable vehicle loading ramps
141 Ramp hydraulic jack
142 Drinking water containers

3 Static dischargers
4 Rudder construction
5 Rudder tab
6 Tail navigation lights
7 Tailcone fairing
8 Elevator tab
9 Port elevator construction
0 Static dischargers
1 Elevator horn balance
2 Tailplane construction

158 Static dischargers
159 Fuel system vent
160 Wing tip fairing
161 Port navigation light
162 Outer wing panel rib construction
163 Port wing integral fuel tank
164 Front spar

C-130 HERCULES

C-130 HERCULES

Arthur Reed

LONDON

IAN ALLAN LTD

Acknowledgements

The author wishes to thank the many people in aviation who found time to talk to him about the Hercules, and in particular Joseph Earl Dabney, and Everett A. Hayes, of Lockheed-Georgia, and members of the Hercules squadrons at Royal Air Force Lyneham, Wiltshire.

First published 1984

ISBN 0 7110 1353 5

United States distribution by

Motorbooks International
Publishers & Wholesalers Inc
Osceola, Wisconsin 54020, USA ®

© Arthur Reed 1984

Published by Ian Allan Ltd, Shepperton, Surrey; and printed by Ian Allan Printing Ltd at their works at Coombelands in Runnymede, England.

Contents

1
Birth of the 'Anyplace, Anytime' Workhorse

With, at the time of writing, over 1,700 ordered by operators in more than 50 countries, and built in over 40 military and commercial versions, the Lockheed C-130 Hercules, variously affectionately known as the 'Herk', the 'Herky Bird' and 'Fat Albert', easily claims the title of the best-selling, and most widely known transport aircraft produced in the West since World War 2.

The type had its roots in that conflict, for it was the inadequacy of the piston-engined transports developed between 1939-45 during the Korean war of the early 1950s, in which jet aircraft fought with jet aircraft consistently for the first time, that produced a demand from the fighting forces of the United States for something more modern to give them battlefield support.

Pentagon thinking was also changing on the strategic level, with the need growing for the transport of large armies of men and their materiel about the world, rather than keeping those armies static for long periods at expensive overseas bases.

The moment of conception for the Hercules can be traced to a meeting called at short notice in the Pentagon during the weekend following the outbreak of the Korean war. Various high-flown and lengthy views on what a new transport might look like were dispensed, but the fog of words was eventually dissipated by a United States Air Force colonel who, short of patience and, presumably, fresh-air in the smoke-filled room, encapsulated the ragged discussion as follows: 'What we need is a medium transport that can land on unimproved ground, be extremely rugged, be primarily for freight transport, have a troop-carrying capability, and carry about 30,000lb over a range of 1,500 miles.'

A GOR — general operational requirement — was issued by the USAF along these lines on 21 February 1951, and RFPs — requests for proposals — followed shortly to Lockheed, Fairchild, Douglas and Boeing. The RFPs called for a 'medium transport to perform tactical and logistics missions — an advanced, all-purpose workhorse type, aerial vehicle that can go anyplace, anytime, without elaborate facility or equipment preparations'.

Each of the companies to which the RFPs were sent had seen the need coming and had prepared their proposals well in advance. So great was the urgency of the time, that the decision to select that from Lockheed was taken, and the contract for the building of two prototypes signed, a mere five months after the RFPs were issued.

With its C-130 design, Lockheed was able to meet most of the parameters outlined in the GOR, which included a requirement to carry 25,000lb of payload to forces holding a bridgehead in enemy territory, a combat radius of 1,100nm, with no refuelling at the bridgehead, and with flight over the combat zone at high speed and down to 1,000ft altitude.

As a resupply vehicle, the successful aircraft type had to carry 37,800lb of freight over 950nm and return without refuelling, or 25,800lb over 1,300nm. As a logistic-support aircraft, the range required was 1,700nm with 37,800lb of cargo, and in the troop-carrying configuration, it had to take 92 soldiers and their weapons, or 64 paratroops.

Willis Hawkins, then head of the Lockheed advanced design department, told his team that what the military wanted was a hybrid mating of the jeep, the truck and the aeroplane. They kept the design and the mock-up simple and rugged, and chose a turbo-prop engine because one of the other main demands of the USAF was operational economy. What emerged was the basic Hercules shape so well-known today, although it has been modified slightly over the intervening 30 or more years, particularly in the area of the nose. It had a high aspect-ratio wing of 132ft span and 1,745sq ft area, with a cargo floor at truck bed level approached through an in-flight operable ramp and door.

So that the floor could be placed at such low level, and so that the Hercules would be able to land on soft fields, the wheels were put in wells on either side of the fuselage, in tandem, with large, low-pressure tyres. A wing-mounted dual-wheel arrangement was considered, but discarded. A four-engine design was chosen to meet the tough engine-out demands which had been tabled by the military.

The engines chosen were Allison T56-A-1As, each producing 3,750shp, linked to variable-pitch, constant-speed propellers to give the Hercules a cruise speed of 360mph, which was faster than the fastest passenger airliners of that era.

The interior design of the fuselage was unusual in that it was not cylindrical, but box-like, a shape which offered space for cargo 41ft long, 10ft wide and 9ft high. Pressurisation was built in, as the new aircraft was to be a troop and casualty-carrier, as well as a freighter.

With the upwards sweep of the rear of the fuselage to provide the room for the loading of large loads up the ramp, the tip of the huge tail fin — huge to give sharp response on low-speed approaches — was 38ft above the ground, while a further unusual feature was a roomy flight deck with no fewer than 23 windows, a big 'greenhouse' which gave a 20deg angle of vision down a striking 'Roman nose' for tactical approaches to rough fields.

The resultant square and pug-ugly look was at total variance with Lockheed's accepted house design, which had produced such sleek types as the Constellation airliner, and the F-80 fighter. When the wraps were pulled off of the large model of the Hercules at the Burbank, California, plant in 1952, there was apparently a long silence, broken by the famed Clarence 'Kelly' Johnson, master of the Lockheed experimental 'skunk works', and father of many of Lockheed's successful designs, objecting to the shape which had emerged. Martin Caidin, in his book, *The Long Arm of America* (E. P. Dutton and Co, New York, 1953) wrote of that occasion, 'The Hercules didn't really rest on the ground; it hugged the concrete and glowered.'

The team that had designed the Hercules explained to their colleagues that while streamlining was in for fighters, the Hercules was to do a rugged, utilitarian job, and would fly for most of its time at low speeds. They pointed out that its tubby shape hid a number of considerable aerospace technology achievements, such as the pressurisation of the entire interior — despite the fact that it had so many doors and other 'holes', the large flight deck, and a big rear ramp — a high-pressure hydraulic system, high-voltage AC electrical

Left: How the Hercules story began: the maiden flight of the first YC-130 which took off in short order from the Lockheed field at Burbank, California, with Stan Beltz and Roy Wimmer at the controls on 23 August 1954. The aircraft was airborne in 800ft. *Lockheed*

Right: 'Roman-nosed' early production C-130As lined up on the flight line at Lockheed-Georgia as production geared up for the USAF. *Lockheed*

Right: C-130 'front office', with its roominess, 40sq ft of glass area, and excellent downwards view, was a dream for transport pilots used to the cramped quarters of earlier types. Pictured are (left) Lloyd Harris, Lockheed chief production pilot, and Don Mills, in an early C-130A. *Lockheed*

Below: Production of Hercules was moved, early in the programme, from Lockheed-California to Lockheed-Georgia. Here, the mock-up is driven through the countryside on low-loaders after being transhipped at the port of Savannah. *Lockheed*

Above: Out on the first flight, the YC-130, tail No 33387, crosses the Sierra Nevada mountain range on its way from the company airfield at Burbank to Edwards AFB. *Lockheed*

system, fully-boosted servo controls to give light, but powerful response, and machined skins with integral stiffening.

Machined panels, including one section 48ft long, were designed for the upper and lower wing surfaces, doing away with much of the riveting which was at that time going into aircraft manufacture, and producing a stronger and stiffer structure. A further new development was the use of around 300lb of titanium for engine nacelles and wing flaps, and high-strength aluminium alloys right through the design. This, and the integral milling of some of the major components, produced a finished product which was up to 10,000lb lighter than some of the competing proposals. Each Hercules was made up of 75,000 parts, but although this sounded a lot, it in fact reversed a trend of the time to go towards more-complicated aircraft. To help it meet the requirement for short-field operation, Lockheed designed in with Allison reverse-pitch propellers, and powerful anti-skid brakes.

Weighing of the first prototype showed that at 108,000lb, Lockheed had beaten its own gross-weight target of 113,000lb by 5,000lb. At the production stage, however, the manufacturers designed back in about 1,000lb in areas where the designers felt the structure needed beefing up. Predicted operating figures bettered all round the minimum requirements which had been laid down by the USAF — cruise speed was 20% up; normal power, ceiling and rate of climb 35% higher, normal power, one-engine-out ceiling and rate of climb 35% better, and 55% faster; take-off distance with maximum power 25% less; landing distance, using brakes only, 40% less.

Lockheed had by this time decided that production of the C-130 should be carried out not in California, but as its Marietta, Georgia, plant, a decision which was coloured by the fact that Marietta had recently produced 394 copies of the six-jet B-47E bomber under licence from Boeing, and at the end of the contract had done the virtually unheard of thing of returning to the US Government several millions of dollars of budgeted funds which remained unspent.

A wooden mock-up of the Hercules, weighing all of 100,000lb, was switched from Los Angeles to Marietta, its marathon journey splitting into two main parts — by sea from Los Angeles, through the Panama Canal, to Savannah, Georgia, lashed to the deck of a US Army ship, and then by road on a low-loader which crawled over 275 miles, through the towns, villages and cotton fields of Georgia, while telephone engineers cut lines to let it through, and children enjoyed a day off school to watch the progress.

Roll-out of the first production model from the Marietta plant came on 10 March 1955, when the state governor, Mr Marvin Griffin, broke a bottle of water from the local Chatthoochee river over the aircraft's nose — at the fourth attempt. Governor Griffin is reported as saying to the assembled Lockheed top brass, 'You build tough airplanes.'

First flight of the Hercules had taken place from Burbank seven months earlier, on 23 August 1954, with Stan Beltz as captain, Roy Wimmer co-pilot, and Jack Real and Dick Stanton as flight engineers. After a postponement to allow the early-morning Los Angeles smog to thin, Beltz took the prototype for two runs along the Burbank runway, just allowing the nose to pitch up, before stopping short, using prop reversal. Two chase 'planes then took off, a P-2V with Kelly Johnson on board, and a B-25 carrying photographers.

Take-off by the lumbering standards of that day was both sprightly and short. The YC-130 was off the ground in 855ft, and after 30deg initial climb, Beltz levelled off at 10,000ft to initiate a series of successful tests on landing gear, control surfaces, and flaps, followed by some stall checks. Landing was a Edwards Air Force base, in the Mojave desert at the back of Los Angeles, after 61min Beltz is recorded as having said when he emerged from the aircraft, 'She's

a real flying machine. I never saw such an eager aircraft.'

First flight of the first production Hercules, that which had been christened by Governor Griffin, took place out of Marietta on 7 April 1955, with the US tail number 53-3129. This time, with Bud Martin and Leo Sullivan at the controls, the unstick distance was 800ft, and by the time it reached overhead the end of the 10,000ft runway, it altitude was 2,500ft. After testing the undercarriage operation over the field at 5,000ft, the crew climbed the aircraft to 10,000ft, and before landing, made two fast runs at 1,000ft above the runway. Sullivan's comment after landing was, 'We knew that here was one of those happy combinations of shape, structure and propulsion system where everything fits together just right.' The crew were right in their assumption, but it took some time before the dream was fulfilled.

Above: YC-130 prototype crew pose for pictures after the maiden flight, at Edwards Air Force Base. Left to right: Jack Real, flight test engineer; Roy Wimmer, co-pilot; Stan Beltz, pilot; Dick Stanton, flight engineer.

Right: Bud Martin and Lee Sullivan, Lockheed test pilots, tell a crowd of interested onlookers how it was shortly after completing the first flight of the first production C-130, on 7 April 1955. *Lockheed*

2
Ironing out the Wrinkles

This was the third flight of the first production machine, and apart from the effect on morale of the Lockheed camp, it put the programme back, because the aircraft was packed with test equipment, which had to be salvaged and installed in aircraft 3011, which was designated as the new structural-test vehicle.

The story had a happy ending, however, for the cause of the fire was quickly identified and fixed, while 3001, despite her woebegone appearance on the Dobbins runway after the fire, covered with foam, and with her port wing sagging, was rebuilt and flew on for many years. It served successively as a space-vehicle tracker on the Atlantic missile range, as a transport, as a gunship in Vietnam, logging 4,500 hours in that theatre of operations alone, and then as a trainer with the USAF Reserve.

The combination of the Allison T-56 engine and the Curtiss-Wright variable-pitch electric propeller posed a far more serious problem, and one that took much longer to fix. The T-56 was an update of the T-38 which Allison had developed for the US Navy, and which had built up a reputation for ruggedness, reliability, and excellent performance at high altitude. It was designed to run at maximum revs under all normal flight conditions, on the ground, on take-off, in flight and on landing (which is the reason for the Hercules' high noise level when taxying), the gradations in power necessary coming from automatic pitch changes of the propellers in response to movements of the throttle. Blade angles constantly switched to maintain the engine at its maximum rpm of 13,820, a major advantage of this principle being that at these revs, the aircraft's generators and fuel-flow system receive a constant and unfluctuating input of power.

It all works well today, but in the development phase it provided countless headaches and sleepless

Between the first flight of the first production Hercules, in April 1955, and the delivery of the first operational aircraft to the USAF in December the following year, a great deal of time was spent by Lockheed, and the air force, in ironing out the wrinkles in the basic design, some minor, others of a major nature, which began to show up as the intensive development programme accelerated.

The first snag to show was a small one, but it resulted in the near writing-off of the first production aircraft, serial No 3001, USAF tail No 33129. Turbulent conditions low down as the aircraft carried out calibration passes of the control tower at Dobbins Air Force Base disconnected a fuel line, causing fuel to spray from the number two engine as the 'plane came in to land. When the props were put into reverse to aid stopping, the engine burst into flames. All of the flight crew evacuated the aircraft safely, and the Dobbins fire crew put the blaze out with foam within 10 minutes of its starting, but by that time the wing with the burning engine on it had snapped.

Left: The first production Hercules suffered a serious fire after landing from a test run, and was doused with foam at Dobbins, the US Air Force Base next to the Lockheed-Georgia works. The incident, due to a loose fuel connection, produced a hiccough in the test programme, but the aircraft was rebuilt and served with the USAF for many years. *Lockheed*

11

nights for the airframe, engine, and propeller experts who were involved.

The trouble was, according to one of the Lockheed engineers working on the programme at that time, 'When the propeller got an electric signal, it would over-compensate on the pitch, and then it would cut back, cut back.' Pilots flying in the development schedule found that the propeller 'grabbed at the air', and changed pitch without giving them warning, with the result that the early Hercules progressed through the skies in a series of starts. One of the test pilots described it as follows: 'You would be surging, perhaps fore and aft, or right and left, but you would never see anything on the gauges, because it would react so fast that there would be no RPM or fuel-flow changes.'

The problem was traced to the reduction gear, which had a nasty habit of melting under stress, and which had a life of only a few hours. Prototype aircraft were returning from test flights with two engines feathered, and there were desperate attempts to make a 'fix' of the trouble, but the whole thing came to a head when, early in 1956, Lockheed and the USAF called a press conference to show off their new air-craft, and the evening before the event was due to take place, the Hercules which was earmarked to be used 'went sick' with two defective props. The defective items were replaced in a rush job during the night, but Lockheed had reached the stage where they could see

Above: The B version of the Hercules gave higher speed and gross weight, and more powerful engines driving the four-bladed Hamilton-Standard propeller, instead of three-bladed Curtiss-Wright props. *Lockheed*

Right: C-130E cruises over the home of the Herks, the Lockheed plant at Marietta, Georgia, with the Dobbins AFB runways in the background. *Lockheed*

12

their entire programme 'going down the drain', as one company executive termed it, if the problem was not beaten.

Test aircraft No 3007 was given over entirely to a project called, 'Let's make the electric prop work', and a second, No 3006, was given over to the testing of a new propeller, hydraulically-operated, which had been produced by Aero-Products, a subsidiary of the Detroit Diesel Allison Division of General Motors.

These two projects rapidly convinced the Lockheed 'top brass' that the Curtiss-Wright electric propeller was not going to be trouble-free in time, and a decision was made to switch to the Aero-Products version, which had been virtually trouble-free from the start. By that time, the Curtiss-Wright had begun to improve, but Lockheed had 49 of its new airplanes lined up without props of any kind, and was not in the mood to wait any longer. These 49 Hercules, all 'A' versions, were retrofitted with the Aero-Products prop.

This worked beautifully, but ironically it was not to be the equipment with which Lockheed stayed. From the 'B' version of the aircraft, the provisions of the pro-

Left: Herks come down the production line at Lockheed's Marietta, Georgia works. In this picture, the centre section, with the centre wing box in place, is about to be mated with the nose. *Lockheed*

Below: Later in the productive cycle, this photo shows completed aircraft, their engines already installed. At the time of writing, over 1,700 C-130s had been ordered. *Lockheed*

mechanism had stripped) and the aircraft was eventually landed, wheels-up, on a carpet of foam.

Despite a shower of sparks as the metal ground along the concrete, there was no fire, and the propeller tips did not strike the ground. Pope AFB patched up the damaged belly with sheet metal, and the Hercules was then flown back to Lockheed-Georgia for permanent repairs. These were completed in 10 days, and the aircraft was returned to the test programme. It was an early example of the ruggedness of the Hercules which was to become such a feature of the aircraft in the years which followed.

One potential problem with the Hercules which the Lockheed engineers identified and solved in advance concerned that of retaining the pressure in the fuselage against the leaks which were possible around the rear cargo door, measuring 9ft by 10ft. The other holes in the fuselage were, two paratroop exit doors, a forward side cargo door, and a crew entry door. The worry was that the rear ramp door would blow out catastrophically when the cabin was pressurised up to 15lb/sq in, and to overcome this possibility, Lockheed devised a system whereby they filled the test Hercules with hundreds of cardboard barrels, each with a small hole drilled in the end.

When the aircraft was pressurised, each of the barrels pressurised also. If the ramp door failed, the air, instead of rushing out in one blast, would be trapped in the barrels, and would emerge in a more controlled form. This is, in fact, exactly what happened on the day of the test. The fuselage pressure was brought up to 12.7lb/sq in, at which point the ramp latches gave way. Barrels were blown out through the hole, but there was no damage, and nobody was injured.

Furthering their pressurisation tests, the Lockheed people took a technical leaf out of the book of the Royal Aircraft Establishment, Farnborough, England, which had built a water-pressure tank in which a fuselage could be submerged in its search for the reason why early Comet airliners had disappeared in flight. Lockheed built a metal box, 40ft high, in which a test aircraft was submerged, with its wings protruding from the sides, and then continually raised and lowered the water pressure to simulate the changes in air pressure encountered by any aircraft on every flight. Once again, any pressurisation explosion could be contained safely, and as a result of this method the problem of the ramp door was found to be metal in the catches which was far too brittle. It was changed, and other minor problems of a similar nature solved, and

peller was thrown open to competition, the winner of which was Hamilton-Standard, with its four-bladed propeller, and it is this piece of equipment which has been fitted to Hercules ever since that day.

One consolation to the Hercules engineers, who were working in teams 24 hours a day, seven days each week, to try to ensure that the company met its delivery date, was that the propeller trouble gave them time to sort out other more minor problems which were showing up. Among these was an undercarriage which refused, on occasions, to come down when cycled. One of these occasions occurred, embarrassingly, when five US Army colonels forming a group which evaluated air-drop systems, were on board out of Pope Air Force Base. Paratroops were dropped, and the aircraft headed back to Pope with the colonels on board.

When the landing gear declined to operate, the pilot suggested to the senior officers that they should bale out, but they pointed out that they had not brought parachutes with them. All efforts to bring the gear down, including manual winding, proved unsuccessful (examination showed later that a part of the screw eventually the test airframe was taken to 200% of the pressure it was likely to find in the air, and passed with colours flying.

Meanwhile, the flying test aircraft were being put through the most straining manoeuvres, including 3g 'upbending' of the wings, by having a full payload in the fuselage, and hardly any fuel in the wing, and negative 1g by putting the aircraft into a 'downbend' with maximum fuel in the wing, and no payload in the fuselage. In such manoeuvres, aircraft plumbing and wiring bent and stretched like banjo strings, but stood up to the strain. In the end, the Hercules emerged from Marietta bound for the USAF with the majority of the technical wrinkles removed, and in the process of this intensive programme, Lockheed-Georgia came of age, moving on from an assembly plant, which it had been in the days of the B-47, to a great aerospace centre whose technological skills enabled it to embark later on demanding projects like the C-141 and the C-5 Galaxy jet-powered freighters.

Above: Early B model out on test: note that this version has the characteristic radar bulge, and has lost the Roman nose. *Lockheed*

Below: Early rough-field take-off and landing tests at Elgin AFB, Florida. The strip used was 2,000ft long, and on some roll-outs after landings, the trials aircraft sank in 20in. *Lockheed*

3
Hercules into Service

The 463rd Troop Carrier Wing of Tactical Air Command became the first unit of the USAF to receive Hercules into operational service, taking delivery of five 'As', fitted with Air-Products propellers, on Sunday, 9 December 1956, at Ardmore, Oklahoma. The aircraft were flown to Ardmore from Marietta, and the first one to touch down was USAF tail No 5023 (Lockheed 3050). The aircraft, named *City of Ardmore*, was greeted on the ramp by a stagecoach pulled by four Shetland ponies, and by General O. P. Weyland, commander of TAC, who said, prophetically, that the new aircraft would, 'play a most-important role in our composite air strike force . . . for it will increase our capability to airlift

engines, weapons, and other critical supply requirements'. Lockheed chairman Robert E. Gross handed the Hercules over on behalf of the manufacturers.

But the first true test of the USAF's new transport came as a result of not some international crisis, but to help the domestic authorities quell trouble at home. A squadron of Hercules was despatched with troops to Little Rock, Arkansas, where there was unrest over the desegregation of schools, from Stewart AFB, Tennessee, and this pattern was soon to be repeated as similar uproar spread in other cities in the south of the USA.

The next call came in May 1958, in response to mob violence which had broken out in Caracas, Venezuela, following a visit there by US Vice President Richard Nixon. President Eisenhower ordered paratroopers to go to standby positions in the Caribbean, and 40 Hercules were used to lift 570 of them and their equipment, overnight from Fort Campbell, Kentucky, to San Juan, Puerto Rico, a distance of 1,600 miles. The troops, with their impedimenta, including 44 jeeps, 22 rocket launchers and a helicopter, went no further than San Juan, for the crisis evaporated as quickly as it had begun, but the airlift was the first real test of the Hercules as a logistic transport, and a forerunner of many such exercises to come.

Later that same year, in July 1958, the Hercules were deployed abroad in a big way for the first time when the President of the Lebanon appealed to the United States for aid following the overthrow of the pro-Western government in Iraq. The operation used

100 Hercules, carrying men and materials from bases in Europe and the United States to Adana, in Turkey. Once again, the crisis faded quickly and the feeling began to grow that one of the reasons for this was the fact that the United States, with the Hercules, was able to react speedily to a flare-up anywhere in the world.

The following month, the US-based Hercules were off at short notice to Ashiya, Japan, with troops and equipment, in the face of the Taiwan Straits crisis, in which the Communist Chinese were shelling the Nationalist Chinese islands of Quemoy and Matsu,

and looking ready to invade. From Japan, the Hercules poured their cargoes into Taiwan, aircraft taking off anything up to five tons overweight, and landing in amongst the Nationalist Chinese fighters, crewed up and waiting for the word to take off.

Once again, with the arrival of the Hercules and their loads, what could have been a world crisis blew over. A similar call came in late 1962, when the Indian nation, whose northeast frontiers were being crossed by the Communist Chinese, appealed for help. President Kennedy assigned 12 Hercules from Evreux,

Left: C-130A with three-bladed props, taxis out at Lakenheath in 1960 after taking part in USAF open day air show.
Brian M. Service

Top: The sparkling, brand-new C-130E Hercules which Lockheed and the USAF flew to the 1963 Paris air show to demonstrate the long-range capabilities of their latest basic version.
Brian M. Service

Above: Sizing up the opposition: a C-130E stares out a Franco-German Transall C-160 freighter at the 1963 Paris air show.
Brian M. Service

17

France, of the 322nd Air Division, and these flew into rough airstrips at high altitude in the Kashmir region of the Himalayas. During the nine months that they remained, the Hercules performed prodigious feats of logistics, moving, for instance, 5,000 troops of the Indian Army over the mountains into the Assam valley in the space of four days. Each journey took $7\frac{1}{2}$ hours, and the Indian soldiers were packed 120 men at a time into the C-130s. The aircraft regularly went into Leh, altitude 10,500ft, although the Hercules manual said at that time it should not be operated into airfields higher than 6,000ft, and largely as a result of their operation, the Indians were able to stave off the Chinese invaders.

Left: Cockpit of one of the later C-130 versions in flight, showing its roominess, and the excellent all-round vision for the crew. *Lockheed*

Below: This C-130B is about to swallow five pallets of cargo at McGuire AFB, New Jersey, in October 1966. *Brian M. Service*

Over the years, the Hercules has been involved in many operations which helped to alter the course of world history — and the Vietnam war was the supreme test — but one of these which must be mentioned is Operation 'Thunderball', the use of C-130s by the Israeli Air Force to rescue 100 Jewish hostages held by terrorists at Entebbe airport, in Uganda. The 100 were among the 243 passengers on an Air France A300 Airbus hijacked soon after take-off from Athens, and forces to fly to Entebbe, where the terrorists were harboured by the despotic Idi Amin, then ruler of the country.

When news reached Israel that the terrorists were threatening to begin killing their prisoners, four IAF Hercules took off on the 3,500km non-stop flight, loaded with troops and warlike equipment — and a black painted Mercedes limousine to resemble that used by Amin. They were escorted by IAF F-4 Phantoms on the first 700 miles of their journey, but after that, they were on their own, although a flying command post, a Boeing 707 painted in El Al Israeli Airlines colours and loaded with electronic counter-measure equipment, had gone on ahead, and was being refuelled in Nairobi.

While the 707 orbited Entebbe, 'snowing' out the control tower radar, the Hercules landed undetected at Entebbe airport, discharged the Mercedes, Land Rovers and heavily-armed troops. The troops stormed the old terminal building, where the hijacked passengers had been kept in the most wretched conditions, cutting down terrorists on the way, blasting a Ugandan army truck which blundered into the area, and blowing up Ugandan Air Force MiG fighters parked on the airport apron. With a minimum of casualties (although the commander of the Israeli force was shot and killed by a sniper), the commandoes led the bewildered hostages to the Hercules, which then each safely took off to fly to Nairobi, where they were refuelled for the flight back to Israel. This was on 4 July 1976, and the rejoicing of the Israel nation was great indeed. One again, the Hercules had proved its value as a tough and dependable carrier of men and materials in the most difficult of conditions — and as a means for nations to write world history.

Above: E model Hercules of the USAF does a low fly-by at RAF Mildenhall. *Lockheed*

Below: Brand-new H model C-130 for the US Air National Guard after being delivered. ANG units in Oklahoma and Mississippi took 16 'Hs' on to their inventory in 1980. *Lockheed*

Three photographs showing a Sheridan being dragged out of the rear end of a USAF Herk during a LAPES drop exercise. The first *(above)* at Fort Bragg, North Carolina shows the aircraft with undercarriage down to reduce speed, and in case of an inadvertent touch on the ground while flying at such a low altitude. The others *(right, below right)* show a LAPES drop during a NATO exercise in West Germany. During these exercises, a C-130 practised landings and take-offs on a German autobahn. *Lockheed (all)*

20

Above: US Air Force Hercules LAPES a small pack of stores, using only one parachute, to a remote station in a snowy landscape, and from a very low altitude. *Lockheed*

Below: C-130F leaps into the air on a short field take off *Lockheed*

4
Herks of many Types

The impact of the high-powered Hercules on USAF aircrews used to flying the old, slow, C-119, was remarkable. In the early days of its service, the trick was to take unwary passengers for a ride, run up the engines to full throttle against the brakes at the end of the runway, release them, and then do a rocket-like take-off, followed by a 40deg climb out. Stories circulated that the C-130 could out-fly the Sabre jet fighter both straight and level and in the turn, and out-climb Canadian T-33s, and all sorts of aerobatics, not generally associated with heavy transport aircraft,

were essayed at high altitude. Demonstration fly-bys on only one of the four engines were not unknown.

All of this culminated in the formation of a Hercules aerobatic team. This was at Ardmore AFB during 1957, and was put together by the 463rd Troop Carrier Wing, using 'A' models. Captains Hubert Chaney, James Akin, David Moore and William Hatfield started filling in days when there were no scheduled operations for the Herks by practising close-formation passes over the airfield, after taking off at five-minute intervals, gradually expanding into more-demanding manoeuvres.

Their 'act', which began as no more than a bit of fun to pass the time, became renowned over a wider area than the base, and before long the 'Thunderweasals', as they were initially called — later being renamed, with rather more style, the 'Four Horsemen' — were being invited to perform in other parts of the United States, and then abroad, from Denmark to Japan. A typical display pattern would be: take-off at two-second intervals, with a roll of less than 2,000ft, with the undercarriages coming up all together; a steep climb-out at 4,000ft/min to cross the end of the runway at 1,500ft, by that time in diamond formation; high-speed passes down the runway in both diamond and arrow-head shapes; and then finally a 'bomb burst', with the aircraft banking away at 45 and 90deg.

C-130 Derivatives

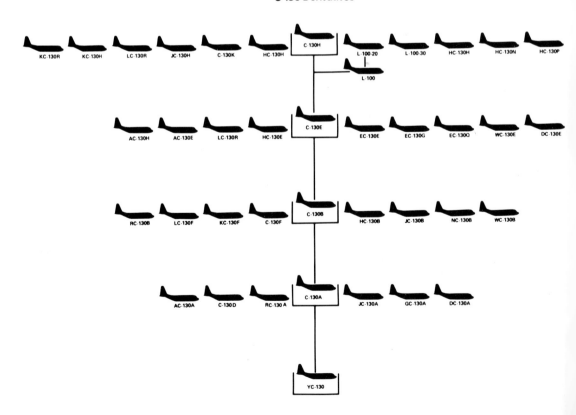

Far left: The Lockheed C-130 Hercules family tree. Stemming from the YC-130 prototype, there have been four main models, the A, B, E and H, and a total of 40 different versions. Top left: This early A model Hercules has the original sloping nose with the small APS42 radar. Fin leading edge is unpainted to speed de-icing from hot air from the engines, and the prop spinners do not have air-cooling hole in the centre, nor black rubber de-icing covers. Centre left: Neat near-plan view of a B version of the C-130 in flight. Note escape hatches forward (above the S in US) and aft (to the left of the fin fillet). Left: Over 500E model Hercules were delivered, 389 of them to the USAF, of which this is a typical example. Peak production rate of the E at Marietta rose to 15 a month as the Vietnam war escalated. Arrival of the E model in quantity enabled USAF to phase out earlier A and B models. Below: One of the Air National Guard's later H models in flight. ANG strength in Hercules was topped up after a number of the force's early models were taken to equip the South Vietnam Air Force during 1972/73. Lockheed (all)

The performances of the 'Four Horsemen' continued, in between their normal duties, like being in attendance at world crises from Taiwan to the Lebanon, until 1960 when, with the 463rd wing absorbed into the 839th Air Division at Sewart AFB, Tennessee, they had their request to be scheduled as an official demonstration team turned down. Soon after that, they disbanded, but by that time the versatility and sheer flyability of the C-130 had been well-proven.

Aerobatic demo team; what next? The answer to that was even more remarkable when the size and weight of the C-130 is considered — landing on board an aircraft carrier. This happened in October 1963, when the US Navy decided that a feasibility study of operating large transport aircraft on to and off 'flat-tops' should be made. The USS *Forrestal* was positioned 500 miles off the northeast coast of the US in heavy seas. The aircraft selected for the task was a US Marines KC-130F tanker, with Lt James H. Flatley III in command. Minor modifications made by Lockheed for the test included installation of an improved anti-skid braking system, and the removal of underwing fuel pods.

In the event, the demo was a great success. Flatley brought the Hercules in towards the pitching deck of the *Forrestal* with a sink rate of 9ft/sec, and reversed propeller thrust when still a few feet away from touchdown. The first landings were made into a 40kt wind. In all, Flatley and his three-man crew, consisting of co-pilot, flight engineer and a Lockheed engineering flight test pilot, made 29 touch-and-gos 21 full-stop

Above: Not just a heavy transport; a C-130H shows the agility which excited fighter pilots when it first came into service, with a steep bank over Washington state. *Lockheed*

Right: The 'Four Horsemen' aerobatic team, formed with Hercules at Ardmore AFB in 1957 after the full performance capabilities of the USAF's new transport were realised. The team performed in the US and overseas in between normal duties, before being disbanded in the early 1960s. *Lockheed*

landings without the benefit of arrester wires, followed by 21 unassisted take-offs at gross weights varying between 85,000 and 121,000lb. At the lower weight, the aircraft ground to a halt in only 270ft which, it was pointed out, was just over double the aircraft's wing-span of 132ft! At full load, 460ft landings were accomplished, while take-off took 745ft. The aircraft had the legend painted on its side, 'Look ma, no hook'.

Flatley received the Distinguished Flying Cross for his role in the demonstration, but there was no happy ending for the Hercules on this occasion, for the Navy resolved that despite the fact that the feasibility of landing such a large aircraft on a carrier deck had been proved, there was no guarantee that it could be done over and over again during routine operations when the conditions might not be so controlled. Replenishing the fleet at sea was therefore carried out by smaller types, but once again the C-130 had given an impressive showing of its ability to be almost all things to all men.

Left: US Navy pilots from the Naval Air Test Centre, Patuxent River, Maryland, flew this KC-130F on to the aircraft carrier *Forrestal* in a series of tests in 1963. At 85,000lb weight, the aircraft came to a halt in 270ft. *Lockheed*

Below: Roaring off the USS *Forrestal* during the 1963 trials, the Hercules used only 754ft of deck when fully loaded. In the trials, the KC-130F made 29 touch-and-gos, and 21 landings and take-offs. *Lockheed*

Right: DC-130H seen during a world record lift of external weight by a turboprop aircraft (44,510lb) in July 1976. *Lockheed*

Below right: A US Navy DC-130A drone director conversion of the Hercules, which is equipped to carry four drones on its under-wing pylons. This particular aircraft, BuAer No 158228, was converted from a C-130D and assigned to Composite Squadron Three (VC-3) at NAS North Island, Ca. *Lockheed*

As the 1960s went by, the USAF and Lockheed began to realise that they had 'got themselves an airplane' which was far more versatile than the logistic transport which had originally been called for, and designed. Different use after different use was invented for it, and a plethora of marks began to roll off the Marietta production line. To name a few: GC-130A, drone launcher; RC-130A, photographic map-making; JC-130B, satellite aerial recovery; HC-130B (originally called SC-130B), US Coast Guard search and rescue; C-130C, experimental boundary-layer control; C-130D, 'A' models modified for skis; C-130E, increased all-up weight, tank for 1,360gal of fuel under each wing; AC-130E, definitive gunship version; WC-130E, airborne met station; KC-130F, US Marines in-flight tanker, or assault version (the tanker version has a tank for 3,600gal in the cargo hold); C-130F, similar to KC-130F, but for the US Navy; LC-130F, ski version for the US Navy, with extra long-range capability to support Antarctic Operation 'Deep Freeze'; C-130H, 'E' version, but with more-powerful Allison engines derated to 4,500eshp; HC-130H, search and rescue version with extended range for US Coast Guard; C-130K, RAF version, known in that Service as C Mark 1 or, with fuselage plug, C Mark 3; HC-130N, special version for recovery of capsules and aircrew; HC-130P,

in-flight refuelling of helicopters capability, and in-flight recovery of parachute loads; EC-130Q, electronic countermeasures version for the US Navy.

Records for distance, height, weight, also began to go as the Herks got into their stride. In addition to the longest flight on a maiden sortie by a civil aircraft (the 25hr 1min of the L-100, mentioned earlier), C-130s established a record for the highest paratroop drop when nine US Marines stepped out at 44,100ft, for the heaviest low-altitude cargo extraction — 50,150lb, and the load came to a halt 700ft after hitting the ground, for carrying the biggest external load — four remotely-piloted drones weighing a total of 44,510lb, and the longest-distance by turboprops, unrefuelled — 8,790 miles from Taiwan to Scott AFB, Illinois. This latter aircraft had 4,500lb of fuel in reserve on landing. In-flight refuelled flights of over 24 hours became common by RAF Hercules during the Falklands war of the summer of 1982 as the aircraft flew to and from Ascension Island, and the record was established by aircraft coded 179 which stayed in the air coping with strong headwinds for an amazing 28 hours and three minutes (previous record by a C-130 was 27hr 45min). Although it is a turboprop, the Hercules has been known to go very fast on occasions — like the flight of the RC-130A between Tucson, Arizona, and Albany, Georgia, which logged an average speed of 541mph

Above: US Navy operates the ski-fitted LC-130R version of the Hercules on behalf of the US National Science Foundation in the Antarctic. The LC-130R is based on the C-130H with 155,000lb gross weight, and the first appeared in 1968, joining the US Navy's earlier ski Herks.

Below: A CL-130R of US Navy squadron VXE-6 *Lockheed*

Above: JATO (jet-assisted take-off) helps a C-130 off the ground in a steep climb angle. The boost was given by eight small rockets (and is also referred to as RATO) with a few seconds' duration. *Lockheed*

Right: Experimental Hercules soars into the sky with the help of a battery of eight rockets, four on each side of the fuselage. One of the main purposes of these trials was to check stresses on the four-bladed Hamilton-Standard propellers, although JATO has been used to help ski-equipped LC-130R Herks out of short Arctic strips. *Lockheed*

over the ground with the aid of a good following jet-stream.

At the same time, the Hercules was building up its reputation for being a safe and 'forgiving' aircraft to fly. Two squadrons of the Royal Australian Air Force amassed over 250,000 flight hours without an accident with their C-130s; VMGR 252 of the US Marine Corps went for 18 years and 204,000 hours to set a safety record in the history of US naval aviation, and in the 'hairy' flying conditions of the Vietnam war, a USAF recovery squadron logged 125,000 hours without a scratch. Such records were established in spite of the fact that the C-130s were operated into conditions which might be thought to be inviting accidents. The 54th Weather Reconnaissance Squadron, USAF, based on Guam, for instance, flew their HC-130s into the eye of typhoons in an effort to bring back data on the causes of these daunting natural phenomena. In 5,000 such sorties in the heart of over 300 tropical storms, and 100,000 hours of flying, the unit never so much as bent one of its aircraft, despite the fact that the conditions of turbulence encountered were among the most severe in the world.

Jet-assisted take-offs have been tried on Hercules, but such was its performance off the runway using its own engines, that the system never widely caught on.

The earliest use was on the original B model at Eglin AFB, Florida, when eight JATO units were fixed beneath the wings to help lift the aircraft, with a gross weight of 135,000lb into the sky. The test was also to assess stress on the newly-fitted Hamilton-Standard four-bladed propellers.

Hercules have appeared over the years with all manner of protuberances on their exteriors. One of the strangest of these was the 'pair of scissors' on the nose of an E version at Pope AFB, North Carolina, used as part of the Fulton recovery system to snatch a man from the ground. The person to be recovered was fixed to a cable, which was then dragged aloft by a balloon. When the Hercules flew over, it was steered into the cable, and its scissors snagged the line, which was then reeled into the open ramp door by way of a special winch. The first person to be snatched into a Hercules by this system was Capt Gerlad LyVere, on 3 May 1966, and later that same day two men were 'rescued'

Below: US Marine Herk gets a lift off the runway with JATO. Pilots had to anticipate and compensate for the moment the rockets cut out. *Lockheed*

by the same aircraft at the same time. They were Col Allison C. Brooks, commanding officer of the USAF Aerospace and Rescue Recovery Service, and Airman Ronald Doll. Each of the forks protruding from the nose of the version of the Hercules, the HC-130H, was 18ft long and constructed of tubular aluminium. Extended, they formed an angle of 60deg and, when not in use, they were stowed along either side of the aircraft's nose. In order that the line trailing from the balloon to the harness fixed to the person waiting to be picked up should not foul the props in the case of a missed pass, lines made of fibreglass were fitted from the aircraft's nose to each wingtip. The system was frequently employed during the Vietnam war, and saved the lives of many crashed airmen.

The other main use for the HC-130H was as a retriever in America's Space programme. Up to two 1,800gal tanks could be fitted inside the fuselage (in addition to the two standard wing-mounted fuel tanks) to increase the range of this version of the Herk by a further 500nm, and a re-entry tracking system was

Top: First live pick-ups of men from the ground 400ft below took place with HC-130H version of the Hercules in 1966. In this picture, the twin prongs used to snag the balloon cable sent up by the rescue are folded back on either side of the nose, and the 'victim' is reeled in through the rear ramp door. A total of 63 HC-130Hs were ordered by the US for search and rescue. *Lockheed*

Above: This HC-130H of the USAF Military Air Transport Service, and wearing the badge of the Air Force Systems Command, was at the 1965 Paris air show. Its blister on top of the fuselage houses tracking radar, and its Fulton recovery system prongs are folded along its nose. *Brian M. Service*

Right: Closeup of the HC-130H nose-mounted forks. *Lockheed*

grafted on inside a big blister on top of the forward fuselage. The tracking system was developed by the Cook Electric Company, and gave a complete 360deg sweep on the horizontal plane, locking on to the UHF signals which were sent out by the Gemini spacecraft as it emerged on re-entry through the ionosphere.

The system then told the crew of the HC-130H of the bearing of the craft. The crew complement was normally 10 — two pilots, a navigator, radio operator, two flight mechanics, two loadmasters and two experts in parachute-rescue techniques. Endurance was around eight hours. HC-130Hs snatched in mid-air all manner of items which had been in space, including packs of data and film, and were involved right through projects Mercury, Gemini and Apollo. The operation was a highly-complicated, but precise one, and 18 of these specialist versions of the Hercules could, with their advanced communications and navigation equipment, provide coverage right round the world across a wide strip on either side of the equator. A total of 43 were produced, but the Aero-

space Rescue and Recovery Service also took 15 HC-130Ns on to its charge. These were very similar to the 'Hs', but did not have the Fulton forks on the nose, nor the internal tankage facility.

Out of the work of the HC-130Hs in recovering downed airmen and pieces of the space programme grew the use of the Hercules for refuelling helicopters, a task which had hitherto been considered highly dangerous to attempt. Sikorsky S-61s in the HH-3C version were acquired by the ARS as part of a plan to reduce the time and the cost of picking up returned astronauts. The combination of Herk and helicopter would, it was thought, replace the sending of large naval task forces to the splash-down areas, and although this scheme never became a reality, the refuelling of HH-3Cs by HC-130Hs was proved practical, and proved a boon in the Vietnam conflict. A total of 20 HC-130Hs were converted into tankers for the HH-3C, and the later HH-3E, Jolly Green Giant, and were designated HC-130P, being fitted with a refuelling pod under each wing, from which trailed

Above: USAF HC-130P tankers (seen here carrying out refuelling) were modifications of HC-130Hs, used to track re-entering space hardware and 'snatch' them from the sky. The 'Ps' were fitted with a refuelling pod under each wing, but the re-entry tracking radar blister, on top of the fuselage, was retained. *Lockheed*

Left: In 1967, two HH-3E helicopters flew nonstop from New York to the Paris air show in 30hr 46min 10.8sec, refuelled nine times in flight by Hercules tankers. *Brian M. Service*

Right: KC-130R seen shortly after take-off; this version was ordered by the US Marine Corps to augment its tanker force. It is based on the EC-130 airframe, with 155,000lb gross weight, and has hanging under the wings external fuel tanks, and refuelling pods. Maiden flight of the original E version of the Hercules was on 25 August 1961. *Lockheed*

the hoses to refuel two helicopters at once. Helicopter refuelling was normally carried out at altitudes between 4,000ft and 5,000ft, with the Hercules flying with lots of flap down and at speeds not much above the stall.

The US Marine Corps had entered the Hercules refuelling business with an evaluation with the A model as early as 1957. For this exercise, the aircraft were fitted with two 500gal internal tanks and refuelling pods under the wings. So successful were these trials that the Marine Corps ordered 46 tankers, designated KC-130F, to give their fighter-bomber force longer range and/or endurance. This version of the Herk was based on the airframe of the 'B', but had a tank in the fuselage with a capacity of 3,600gal, from which fuel could be transferred into 'customer' aircraft at a rate of 300gal/min through the wing-mounted pods. Flight crew stations were increased to five, and two refuelling-observer positions were installed in the fuselage. All of these modifications to the basic airframe of the Herk were quickly removable, however, so that the aircraft could be returned in short order for use as a basic transport. The US Navy, in fact, bought seven of this version as transports, designating them C-130F. A number of further tanker Herks ordered later by the Marine Corps were based on the basic 'E' Hercules version, and were designated KC-130R.

Ski versions of the Hercules were designated C-130D by the USAF and C-130BL (later LC-130F) by the USN, although the Navy also procured LC-130Rs, three of which were flown in the Antarctic for the National Scientific Foundation. Two LC-130Fs were also flown on behalf of the Foundation, and to

take readings of the surface of the earth as it is below the Greenland ice, one of these was modified to carry additional VHF radars, the aerials being carried underwing.

A further Herk type operated by the USN was the C-130G, taken into the inventory to support the nuclear submarine force. As such, they were packed with specialist radio equipment which enabled them to be used as airborne relay posts to and from the subs cruising beneath any of the world's oceans. These aircraft were designated EC-130G later, and later still were augmented by Hercules with more sophisticated equipment and better accommodation for the crew. The designation EC-130Q was given to this version.

Not surprisingly, the US Coast Guard was an enthusiastic early client for the Hercules. Its first purchases were designated SC-130B, later altered to HC-130B, and the aircraft gave the Service an aerial platform with which it could carry out low-level over-water searches across 1,000nm, and of 7.5 hours duration. Stations on the HC-130B are provided for two pilots, an operations' commander, navigator, and

Above right: TACAMO C-130Q of the US Navy trails two aerials from its tail and underside. The C-130Q is packed with sophisticated equipment and provides airborne communications centre for the US submarine fleet. *Lockheed*

Right: Hercules found a large world market as a maritime-patrol aircraft, because of its long loiter time and because it provided a steady platform low down for aerial photography. It is now extensively used off the south-east coast of the US against drug smugglers. *Lockheed*

systems engineer, while two places are also provided in the fuselage for scanning through the large observation door. For special operations, a command cabin seating 14 can be wheeled into the cargo compartment, and seats can be provided in the compartment itself for up to 44. The USCG also took HC-130Es and HC-130Hs (although the latter were without the parachute-retrieval forks), and one EC-130E, modified for radar calibration, on to its inventory.

Coast Guard Hercules are operated down to as low as 50ft above the water on patrol duties, which have in latter years included spotting drug smugglers off the southern coasts of the USA. The aircraft fly low over suspected drug-carrying ships to photograph their name and home port painted on the hull, and this information is then fed into the computers of the US Drug Enforcement Agency, in Miami. Missions have lasted up to 14 hours at a time, with the aircraft loitering on two of their four engines. USCG crews on board the Hercules use gyro-stabilised binoculars to help them identify boats, whose lettering may be only 12in high. In one incident off Miami, the crew of a suspected vessel were seen throwing brown bales of marijuana overboard as the Coast Guard Herk came in low to 'buzz' them.

Below: US Coast Guard HC-130H has the Fulton recovery system nose forks removed. This version is based on the HC-130B, which has a flight-deck crew of six, and scanning stations with a wide area of visibility in the cargo compartment. Duration is $7\frac{1}{2}$ hours at low altitude with a search radius of 1,000 miles. *Lockheed*

The very first of the long line of Hercules variants which have been produced over the lifetime of the aeroplane was the RC-130A, jointly developed by Lockheed as the Air Photographic and Charting Service of the USAF for aerial survey work. Its equipment included an electronic high precision ranging and navigation triangulation system, a number of cameras, and a photographic darkroom, as well as a facility for dropping sondes to measure wind direction and speed. Later RC-130As which were given extra equipment, such as externally-mounted searchlights, were re-designated RC-130S.

Temco Aerosystems Division of Ling Temco Vought modified 11 C-130As into JC-130As for use in supporting space activities from the Kennedy Space Center, Florida. The aircraft were used to gather information from missiles fired from the range, and also from the nose cones of space capsules after they had re-entered the earth's atmosphere. Endurance was increased to around 12 hours with extra fuel tanks, and large windows were installed in the cabin for spotting returning space hardware. To give safe clearance between the underside of the aircraft and the ground during take-off and landing, some of the additional aerials fitted to this version were made retractable.

Early work on carrying drones underwing was done with modified A models designated GC-130A, and later DC-130A, and successful control of these pilotless aircraft was carried out from the Herks up to 250 miles distant. This work had its fulfilment during the Vietnam war when DC-130Es regularly flew towards enemy lines with two drones beneath each

wing and, after release, directed their flight. The drones collected valuable information by camera over North Vietnam and also, it is assumed, over the Chinese border, before being directed back for a landing behind US lines by their airborne mentor.

The USAF modified six B model Herks into the JC-130B designation as back-up for the Discoverer military space research programme, during which capsule-recovery techniques were developed. The WC-130Bs used by the US for various forms of 'hurricane hunting' and 'typhoon chasing' — in more prosaic terms, weather monitoring, are of a similar standard to the JCs, but have had their on-board met detection and recording equipment upgraded over the years, so that it now includes computers which process the data as it comes in.

Two 'one-off' Herks of note were the NC-130B, which was modified specially to evaluate boundary-layer control, and which was fitted with a pair of Allison T56 engines outboard of its normal four engines, to provide compressed air, and the KC-130F which acted as a support aircraft for the US Marines'

aerobatic team, the Blue Angels. Named *Fat Albert*, it was painted in one of the most startling liveries worn by any of the 1,600-plus Herks produced so far, royal blue underside and tail fin, white top, and a bright yellow cheat line and radar nose. The NC-130B programme was not pursued on the grounds of economy by the USAF (it had cost over £2million when it was dropped by the air force), but was continued by Lockheed, and then by NASA. In 1961, the development aircraft flew non-stop from Marietta to the Paris air show.

A further use for the Hercules has been as an aerial firefighter, a role which was first demonstrated during tests at Edwards AFB during 1971. Following these, and further trials in Arizona two years later, the US Forest Service acquired a number of pallets containing MAFFS, which stands for modular airborne fire-fighting system, and positioned them in areas of the country where the fire risk is great. The MAFFS pallets can be loaded on board Hercules in 10 minutes and their contents, some 3,000gal of fire-retardant liquid nitrate, dumped on a blaze within the space of

Below: C-130 in fire-fighter role dumps 3,000gal of liquid nitrate fire-retardant compound in the space of 10sec. The liquid also contains a fertiliser to help the forest grow again. The Hercules is from the US Air National Guard. *Lockheed*

10 seconds. The nitrate compound also acts as a fertiliser to help the devastated area grow again after the fire has been extinguished.

Providing such a stable aerial platform, the Hercules became a 'natural' for map-making work, and the aerial photography upon which that exact science is based. All manner of advanced and delicate cameras were installed in various C-130s, entailing modifications to the airframe. The RC-130A was given a television blister beneath its nose, and with the use of this and other similar devices, the crews of the Hercules discovered that Cuba, on standard charts, was actually misplaced by 1,200ft, that Iceland was 600ft out, and that the Grand Bahamas Island was actually six miles adrift.

The HC-130H for the US Coast Guard was given massive glass doors on either side of the fuselage through which wide-ranging scanning could be carried out as the aircraft patrolled on sea-rescue, search, iceberg and pollution-monitoring missions. Iceberg patrols entailed 'bombing' bergs with dye so that scientists could chart their tracks. The C-130H-MP version as bought by Indonesia had installed special maritime equipment, including a rest module for crews, a ramp pallet holding rescue kits, flare launcher, loudspeaker, rear-looking observer station, and a specially modified telephoto camera linked electronically to the aircraft's computerised navigation system. The on-board computer provided a printout superimposed over photographs of surface targets, giving precise latitude and longitude, as well as date and time.

Left: This early B model Hercules was used by the NASA Ames Research Centre for numerous different research programmes, including earth survey, in which role it is seen here after touching down on a frozen runway in the Polar region. *Lockheed*

Right: A basic HC-130B US Coast Guard Herk 'bombs' an iceberg with dye so that its progress through the ocean can be marked. This version was originally designated R8V-1G, then SC-130B. *Lockheed.*

Below: Air National Guard Herk casts a beady eye over a cabin cruiser while out on a search and rescue mission. ANG units originally received early A and B version C-130s when the USAF re-equipped with later models. *Lockheed*

5
Workhorse of the Vietnam War

It is no exaggeration to say that without the Hercules, the Vietnam war could not have taken place from the American point of view. The aircraft was indispensable, as a general-duties mover of men and supplies — a 'trash-hauler' as the military described it — in a country with virtually no railways and roads worth mentioning; as a paratroop dropper, as a weather-reconnaissance ship, as a rescue vehicle for downed aircrew, as a medical evacuation ambulance, as a command headquarters, as a tanker, as a gunship, as a drone launcher, and in many other guises too many and too esoteric to mention.

In Vietnam, the Hercules was flown into and out of strips with lengths and surfaces which were impossible according to the book, pulling up in 2,000ft with a light load, in 3,500ft if heavily laden with anything up

to 130,000lb gross weight. Two and a half years after the Vietnam conflict began, the Hercules, backed by other USAF freighter types, had shifted over $2\frac{1}{3}$ million tons of men and materials, so breaking the previous sustained airlift record under combat conditions established during the Berlin blockade crisis of 1948-49. According to one US Army colonel, the C-130 was the 'make-or-break' factor in the Vietnam war — 'If it had been grounded, there is little doubt that the war would have ended. It's as simple as that.'

Stores were delivered in a variety of ways as the conflict went on, and conditions changed. In the early days, LAPES (low-altitude parachute extraction) was the norm, but as the Vietcong moved in closer to the US bases, and began to shoot up the low-flying Hercules with their mortars and heavy machine guns, so the aircraft were forced to fly higher and 'CDS' the stores in, by parachute from heights of up to 10,000ft, but with a high degree of accuracy. When things on the ground became really 'hairy', with the Vietcong in close attendance, and when CDS was not possible because of the weather, or because terrain made a high-level drop impossible, a system called GPES (ground proximity extraction system) was employed. Whereas in the LAPES system, parachutes were deployed to haul the load out of the opened rear door as the aircraft flew across the drop zone at minimal height. GPES used a cable strung across the zone, and a hook hanging out of the back of the Hercules, which would catch on the cable, and yank the whole load out of the back. It was a rough-and-ready system exactly suited to the tough conditions in Vietnam, and the captain of the aircraft would know when he was low

Left: The Vietnam war provided the Hercules with its biggest test to date, and the aircraft came through with flying colours in a bewildering number of roles, but particularly as a 'trash-hauler' (seen here) keeping the troops on the ground supplied. Supplies brought in by Herks played a major part in the victory of the US Marines at Khe Sanh, enabling them to hold out against enormous odds. *Lockheed*

Above: Hercules carried many thousands of troops into areas of Vietnam impossible to reach by any other form of transport. *Lockheed*

Below: Dramatic picture shows a Herk LAPES-ing (low altitude parachute extraction) a load of stores under battlefield conditions. *Lockheed*

Left: Hercules came into their own as tankers during Vietnam, refuelling the Jolly Green Giant HH-3E and other helicopters, which were then able to fly on into North Vietnam to rescue downed US pilots. Here, an HC-130P gives a drink to an HH-3E, and trails a second pipe. The US lost a total of 53 C-130s of various types during the Vietnam war. *Lockheed*

Right: US Marine Corps KC-130 tanker tops up a Super Sea Stallion helicopter. *Lockheed*

enough, because the hook had a microphone attached to it, connected to the pilot's headset so that he could hear when the equipment was dragging along the ground.

In addition to operating over the battle zone, the C-130s went into enemy territory as a propaganda weapon, dropping, it is estimated, over a billion leaflets urging the natives to give up. They also acted as tankers across the Pacific, nurturing US Marine and Navy fighter formations as they headed for the war.

Both in the air and on the ground, the Hercules took an enormous amount of punishment, and at least 35 were written off, it is estimated. But others survived despite tremendous damage, flying out of beleagured airstrips, into which they had delivered vital ammunition and medical supplies, with shell holes plugged by pieces of wood, sometimes with an engine unserviceable, or on fire. Overweight, according to the book, landings and take-offs were routine. If an engine would not start, there was no time to take it to pieces and see what was wrong. Often, a second Hercules would be positioned in front, and the blast from its whirling props would be sufficient to start up the dead motor. And if that did not work, the pilots would take off with three, and hope that the momentum down what passed for the runway would be sufficient to give the vital spark.

Not all the tasks given to the Hercules in Vietnam worked. There was, for instance, the project dreamed up by headquarters for the aircraft to drop chips of soap and detergent along the Ho Chi Minh trail, the main supply route for the Vietcong from North Vietnam to the south, on the assumption that in the rainy season this would brew up the whole area into a froth of lather, making it impossibly slippery for even the most nimble-footed packhorse to pass. Not surprisingly, the scheme was a flop. Nor did a further similar scheme, under which the Hercules dropped silver and lead iodine particles into clouds over the trail, and in areas of Laos, in the hope that this would produce rain, which would, in turn, make the life of the Vietcong unbearable, work any better.

Project 'head shed' was, however, highly successful. This employed Hercules fitted out as aerial command posts, packed full of radios, teletypewriters, voice and data recorders, and a crew of 15 men, which would orbit the battlefield listening out, and giving instructions, directing artillery fire, fighter strikes, and rescue operations for crashed US pilots. EC-130E aircraft had a specially-built airborne battlefield communications and control centre capsule slotted into the fuselage, in which the commander and his staff sat at prepared positions, overseeing the action on the ground 15,000ft or more below. At least one such air-

craft is believed to have been lost in the Iranian desert in April 1980, during President Carter's courageous but unsuccessful attempt to rescue the American hostages from the revolutionary regime of Khomeni.

The post on an AC-130 gunship over Vietnam needing the most nerve was that of the IO, or illuminator operator, otherwise known as the vertical observer who, wearing a helmet and survival equipment, hung over the rear ramp in a harness, watching the ground fire, warning the flight crew of incoming missiles, and telling them which way to take avoiding action.

In its AC-130 version, the Hercules ceased to be a 'non-combatant', and became very aggressive indeed. Armament, mainly used for attacking Vietcong supply trains on the Ho Chi Minh and other trails at night, steadily increased from the original Pave Pronto modification programme, through the Pave Spectre and Pave Spectre 11 programmes, which produced the AC-130E and AC-130H, until the ships bristled with an armoury of weapons, ranging from 7.62mm miniguns, through 20mm and 40mm, to the mighty 105mm cannon.

AC-130s were also equipped with sophisticated sensing devices, both offensive and defensive. Sensors fitted on the aircraft could detect trucks on the trail below, and when two pips on the gunsight coincided,

the shooting commenced. At the end of the Vietnam war, it was estimated that the Hercules gunships had, in their night-time operations, destroyed more enemy material than any other aircraft types in the US inventory. Some of the explosions which it produced on the ground would rock the gunships as they loitered at 150mph, but because they were low and slow, and because fighter cover could not always be provided, the loss rate was also heavy — and each AC-130 carried a crew of up to a dozen. Later E models were fitted with armour plate for the crew, as a result of which the chances were better than in the original AC-130As.

Crews of the gunships, and of all other Hercules types operating over Vietnam, looked particularly keenly for the Soviet-built 'Strella' surface-to-air missiles which were used against US aircraft. The 'Strella' was heat-seeking, and would home in on the rear of the Hercules' engines. It was the job of the IO on the gunships, hanging out the back on his harness, to warn of its approach, but however hard the Hercules jinked, it was hard to throw off the missile when it was working well. In time, the USAF came up with a decoy flare which crews could eject from the back of the aircraft when they saw a 'Strella' on the way towards them. This generated a heat patch behind the Hercules, on to which the missile would turn, while the

41

C-130 went on its way, if not rejoicing, with a very relieved crew.

Crews of 'ordinary' Hercules took a leaf out of the book of the famed IOs, and on their way back to base after a supply or paratroop-dropping mission, would don the restraint harness, have the flight crew lower the rear ramp, and then lean out at crazy angles to wave to the local populace working in the paddy fields. This was a little light relief in a particularly bloody war where that commodity was singularly lacking. A little more of it came from the annual visits to the Servicemen fighting there by Bob Hope and his team of entertainers, and even then the Hercules played their part. Hope and his troupe were usually allocated two C-130s as their transport while touring the theatre of operations, and and aircraft took them into and out of short airstrips just behind the firing line. En route, rehearsals would be held in the back of the flight deck, while everybody enjoyed the in-flight service of coffee and doughnuts. Flying over the war zone on one Christmas eve, Hope and his companions decorated a Christmas tree. Emerging down the Hercules' built-in

airstairs, Bob swung his golf club, put his tongue firmly in his cheek, and commented; 'The crew that brought me here, they're a happy-go-lucky bunch — happy they got it off the ground, and lucky they got it down again.'

'But they're a professional group, and our flight was without incident. The only thing that bothered me was when the navigator couldn't find the cockpit.'

There were other uses for the ubiquitous Hercules in Vietnam — flare-dropping to light up an area at night so that rescue helicopters could home in on a crash in some remote jungle clearing in the hope of saving the aircrew, carrying the battlefield illuminations system — two pods containing 28 lamps producing a total candlepower of 6.14million (the RC-130S version), refuelling Jolly Green Giants, and other helicopters, and carrying beneath its wings Ryan Firebeedrones which could be programmed for both reconnaissance, electronic countermeasures, and attack. But the activity in the final stages of the war, when the US was leaving the theatre of operations, which hit the world headlines was as a carrier of refugees.

Above right: AC-130 gunships were used at night to shoot up North Vietnamese traffic using supply trails towards the south of the country. Pictured is an early A model Hercules in action. *Lockheed*

Right: Herk gunship displays a selection of its formidable armament. Later E model conversions carried heavier weapons and armoured plates for the crew of 13. *Lockheed*

Earlier in the conflict, there had been reports of pro-digious numbers of people being carried in single Hercules, but an all-time record was established in April 1975 when no fewer than 452 packed on board a C-130 out of Tan Son Nhut air base, including 32 on the flight deck, as the Vietcong arrived on the base perimeter. So heavy was the aircraft that it finally became airborne only on the overrun of the 10,000ft runway. Three and a half hours later, the Hercules made a perfect touchdown at a base in Thailand, a feat which was made all the more remarkable by the fact that it had been flown by only one pilot, a Major

Top: AC-130A gunship. *Lockheed*

Above: Pilotless drones used in the Vietnam war to fly over enemy territory and bring back information were carried towards their targets under the wings of the Hercules. Version modified for this work was coded DC-130. *Lockheed*

Phuong, of the Royal Vietnamese Air Force. It was estimated that, with the 452 on board, the Hercules took off some 20,200lb over-weight, and that was assuming that each 'passenger' on board weighed only 100lb on average.

6
Fifty Foreign Air Forces

At the latest count when this book was being prepared, 50 armed forces outside the United States operated the Hercules, a remarkable record, involving some 600 aircraft. The most popular choice among these foreign operators has been the C-130H version, although there are a few 'As', 'Bs' and 'Es' about, and the stretched C-130H-30, based on the RAF C Mk 3, is beginning to make an appearance. Several air forces also operate the L-100 series, the civil version of the Herk. By far the largest majority of the Hercules sold abroad have been configured for the straight transport role, although a few of the more esoteric uses devised for the Herk in service with the armed forces of the United States have crept in. Indonesia, for instance, operates the maritime patrol version, Saudi Arabia a version for

transporting VIPs, and also one which is a flying hospital, and Egypt the EC-130H electronic intelligence gathering version. A number of countries have the KC-130 tanker version in their fleet, while the Royal Air Force, biggest foreign operator, with an initial requirement for 66, converted 16 C Mk 1s with probes for in-flight refuelling, and a further four as tankers (also with probes) during the Falklands crisis.

The most-recent purchases of Hercules by foreign customers have included a C-130H-30 by the Republic of Cameroon to add to the two 'straight' C-130Hs already in its fleet, and which were acquired in 1977. As an example of the dual military/civilian role played by the Herks in service with many of the smaller nations which have bought the type, the Cameroon AF aircraft also operate on behalf of CAMAIR, the country's national airline in both the cargo and passenger role. In the latter configuration they haul 100 people at a time, from football supporters to Moslem pilgrims going to the Haj. Cameroon's Herks, which are among those of 15 African nations which have bought the type, have also been pressed into the carrying of 35,000lb loads of building materials from Paris and Marseilles, France, for government construction in the towns of Maroua and Yaounde.

Hercules total sales topped the 1,700 mark early in 1983 with purchases of C-130Hs by the Japanese Defence Agency, and Dubai, a United Arab Emirate Air Force country, which added a second stretched 30 'Super Hercules' to the L-100-30 already in its fleet. Japan signed for two 'Hs', to add to the two already in its fleet. The Kuwaiti Government bought four of the

Right: RAF station Greenham Common, England, was the scene of possibly the greatest Hercules 'meet' of all time in the summer of 1979. It was the 25th anniversary of the type's first flight, and 15 nations sent a total of 27 Herks of many versions. The *concours d'élégance* trophy was awarded at the meeting to a Royal New Zealand Air Force C-130H-115-LM, even though the aircraft was one of the longest-serving on show, having been delivered in 1964, and having over 10,000 airframe hours.
Brian M. Service

Above left: The Venezuelan Air Force has seven H model Hercules in its inventory. *Lockheed*

Left: Their unusual desert camouflage scheme differentiates the six Hercules C-130Hs in the Sudanese Air Force fleet. *Lockheed*

Below: Twelve H version Herks were bought by the Spanish Air Force, including some KC tanker versions. *Lockheed*

Right: A Republic of Singapore Air Force Herk; inventory lists four C-130s of B and H versions. *Lockheed*

L-100-30 versions in a deal worth $90 million in 1982, having originally bought two L-100-20s in 1971. As has been the case with many of the overseas deals, Lockheed contracted at the same time as the L-100-300 contract was signed to give technical support for the aircraft, flight crew and maintenance crew training, and training equipment back-up, for a period of two years until the new 'planes were totally assimilated into the purchaser's fleet.

The long succession of overseas orders for the Herk was begun in 1958 when the Royal Australian Air Force received 12 'A' versions under the provisions of the US Military Assistance Programme. No 36 Squadron began to put them into service that December, and over the succeeding years the RAAF built up a superb operational record with its aircraft, adding 12 'E's and 12 'Hs'. The Service's A squadron (No 36) and E squadron (No 37) passed the 250,000 safe flying hours point after the aircraft had been in the inventory for 20 years, despite the fact that during that time the C-130s were involved in what the RAAF described as 'hair-raising' situations. No 37 Squadron, for instance, landed aircraft by the light of kerosene flares at night on the devastated Darwin airport in the aftermath of Cyclone Tracy, while flying in the highlands of Papua, New Guinea, where the conditions are among the trickiest in the world, is routine. Scores of mercy flights have also been carried out by 37 into and out of remote spots such as Noumea, and Christmas Island, with medical crews performing operations in transit. Other squadron achievements with its Herks have included, being the first with an Australian aircraft after World War 2 into China, flying in livestock, and later bringing out valuable archaeological exhibits. RAAF Hercules also played their part in support of the Australian forces fighting alongside the Americans in the Vietnam war, with heavy commitments to re-supply and aero-medical evacuation.

After the RAAF, the only other user of the original A model Hercules was the South Vietnam Air Force, which received 32 aircraft which were withdrawn at short notice from the US Air National Guard and Air Force Reserve. This was in late 1972, under a project called 'Enhance', designed to strengthen the South Vietnamese forces as the US prepared to withdraw. Out of 230 B model Hercules which were built by Lockheed, 29 were earmarked for foreign operators under the Military Aid Program, or by direct buy. Ten of these went to the Indonesian Air Force, entering service with No 31 Squadron in 1963; a further seven went to No 28 Squadron of the South African Air Force; four to No 435 Squadron of the Royal Canadian Air Force; four to the 50th Transport Wing of the then Imperial Iranian Air Force; and four to No 6 Squadron of the Pakistan Air Force (which later acquired the four Iranian Bs, plus two of the original L-100 civil version Hercules which had been acquired by Pakistan International Airlines). The Colombian Air Force later took three 'Bs' via Lockheed after the Royal Canadian Air Force had retired its aircraft to buy 'Es' and then 'Hs', and the Royal Jordanian Air Force was provided with two former USAF 'Bs', before acquiring at a later stage four C-130Hs.

It was the launching by Lockheed in the early 1960s of the E model Hercules to meet a shortage of transport aircraft in the USAF Military Air Transport Service that really opened the floodgates of the export market. Orders began to roll in, one of the first being that from the Australians for a second squadron. Argentina signed up for three, Turkey eight, Sweden two, Saudi Arabia nine, equipping Nos 4 and 16 Squadrons, Iran 28, Peru four, Brazil 11, and Canada 24, to equip Nos 435 and 436 Squadrons. A few of these customers received Herks under the US Military Assistance Program, and in some cases these aircraft supplied were designated C-130M. Twelve 'Es' which

were despatched to the Israeli Air Force were former USAF aircraft, rather than newly-built.

But if the E model opened the floodgates abroad, it was the 'H' which broke the dam. With its improved performance, it became at once attractive as a tactical transport to air forces all over the world, and from 1966 onwards orders came in from near and far. While existing customers added to their fleets, new Hercules purchasers included, Nigeria, Malaysia, Denmark, Chile, Libya, Abu Dhabi, Morocco, Spain, Venezuela, Zaire, Norway, Italy, New Zealand and Belgium. Since this early spate of orders, other countries which have taken on the 'H' are, Algeria, Bolivia, Cameroon, Denmark, Ecuador, Egypt (a follow-on order for 14 C-130Hs in 1978 gave Egypt, with a total of 23, the seventh-largest fleet of Herks being operated outside the US), Gabon, Greece, Japan, Niger, Oman, Philippines, Portugal, Singapore, Spain, Sudan, Thailand, United Kingdom, Venezuela and, North Yemen.

Hercules of the 50 foreign customers are used for a multitude of different tasks, and in some cases have been, and still are, engaged in support of 'hot' military activities, from wars to border incursions. The Herks of the Royal Thai Air Force, for instance, ferry supplies to that country's forces engaged in repelling raids across the eastern border by the Vietnamese People's Republic, while two C-130H-30 stretched versions will be employed in counter-insurgency operations. The Royal Australian Air Force sends its Hercules to the Sinai, Egypt, in support of United Nations peace-keeping troops, while the Royal New Zealand Air Force has ferried a small team to operate with the RAAF there.

Morocco's Hercules have been actively engaged in border skirmishes with the Polisario guerillas in the western Sahara, and one is known to have been shot down by a shoulder-launched SAM-7 surface-to-air

Above: One of the Royal Thai Air Force's three H model Hercules, used as transports. The air force has two more 'Hs' in the stretched 30 version for use as counter-insurgency support against incursions across the eastern border by the Vietnamese People's Republic. *Lockheed*

missile. Algeria was given its six C-130Hs as a present by the United States as recognition of the peacemaking role which that country played in the long-drawn-out negotiations with the revolutionary government of Iran towards the release of the American hostages, while the Hercules of the Argentinian Air Force were actively engaged in the Falklands war, both in ferrying supplies from the mainland to Port Stanley until its recapture by the British, and as makeshift bombers. In the Falklands campaign, both sides were using Hercules, and there was a very real danger of mistaken identities.

Herks were used to drop bombs during the Vietnam campaign, but mainly in this case to produce clearings in the forest which could be used as helicopter landing pads. In the Indo-Pakistan war of 1965, however, they were pressed into service by the Pakistan Air Force as bombers against Indian troop concentrations, and 14 such attacks, dropping up to 22,000lb of 1,000lb bombs in each sortie, were made before the ceasefire. As the Herk is limited to a speed of 150kts with its rear cargo ramp open, and at this speed, it was considered, it would be a sitting target for small arms fire as it dropped its load, the PAF set about modifications designed to increase the rate of its bombing run to 280kts. This was achieved largely by removing the lower portion of the cargo ramp. The bombs were rolled out of the rear door in the same way as stores, each attached to a small parachute, and encased in

47

plywood containers standing on pallets of the same material. By the end of the campaign, the PAF estimated that its Herks had delivered 264,000lb of high explosive with an accuracy, without the benefit of bombsights, of anything between 100yd and one mile of the targets. PAF Herks were also heavily committed during the conflict in the transport and troop/paratroop-carrying roles.

Civil versions of the Hercules are now operated by the governments of 11 countries, as well as by commercial operators, and are to be found at airports all over the world on supply missions. The classic peripatetic intercontinental Herk is probably Transamerica Airlines' L-100-30 N19ST which, early in 1983, became the first of all the 1,700 aircraft in this family to pass the 50,000 flight hours milestone. This, Lockheed's statisticians worked out, was the equivalent of 17million statute miles, or 739 trips around the world at the equator — or more than five years in the air.

N19ST became, in 1977, the first Hercules to pass the 30,000 hours mark. It was sold originally by Lockheed as a standard-length L-100 civil version of Delta Air Lines in 1966, and that airline sent it back to the manufacturers two years later to stretch it 8.3ft into the dash 20 configuration. Saturn Airways subsequently acquired the 'plane and had it stretched an additional 7ft to become a dash 30, in 1974. At that time, the Hercules and accumulated 19,492 hours in the air. In late 1976, Saturn and Transcontinental Airlines merged, and subsequently TIA was renamed Transamerica. N19ST is one of eight L-100s which Transamerica assigned to the United States Defence Department LOGAIR and QUICKTRANS cargo routes which criss-cross the US seven days a week with military spares. The dash 30s carry up to 48,000lb of cargo on either single pallet or cargo-train configurations, and their freight loads include complete helicopters and aircraft engines, including those of the Lockheed C-5 Galaxy, the world's largest aircraft.

Below: One of eight C-130E Herks of the Turkish Air Force, finished in its natural metal, plus insignia. Later aircraft wore camouflage. *Lockheed Corporation*

Above: Two C-130Hs are in service with the Sultan of Oman's Air Force, which was formed with British help in 1959. The aircraft play an important role as transports in the expansion of the SOAF, which includes the formation of a second squadron of Anglo-French Jaguar bombers. *Lockheed*

Right: With its STOL performance into short, snow-bound strips, the Hercules was a natural choice for the Royal Norwegian Air Force, which operates six of the H version as transports. Norway is a founder member of NATO, and her aircraft are assigned to Allied Forces Northern Europe. *Lockheed*

Below right: The Federal Nigerian Air Force has six C-130Hs, which share the transport role with Dutch Fokker F27-400s. Originally drawing most of its aircraft from the Soviet Union, the FNAF has recently 'shopped' for aerospace goods in the West, and spent $850million on defence in that area in 1981. *Lockheed*

50

Above: As a former French colony, Niger operates largely French military aircraft, but has two H model Hercules which are used by the Force Arienne du Niger in a joint civil-military transport role. *Lockheed*

Below: The Kiwi bird emblem within the roundel proclaims this a Royal New Zealand Air Force C-130H, one of five operated in the transport role, along with two Boeing 727s. RNZAF has seven operational squadrons. It has a support unit in Singapore, and sent a small team to operate with the Royal Australian Air Force in the Sinai. *Lockheed*

Top: A US Air Force C-130H pictured at low-level; on its fuselage and upper surfaces the aircraft sports the two-tone green and tan colour scheme that was the standard camouflage on USAF tactical aircraft until the late-1970s. *Lockheed Corporation*

Above: US Marine Corps KC-130F Hercules, BuAer No 148890, pictured at MCAS Yuma, Az, in April 1961. A tanker/transport version of the C-130B equipped with underwing refuelling pods, the KC-130F was supplemented in the USMC inventory by the KC-130R tanker version of the C-130H; this particular machine carries the QB fin code of Marine Aerial Refueling/Transport Squadron Three Five Two (VMGR-352). *US Marine Corps*

Top right: A C-130E, s/n 70-1259, of USAF Military Airlift Command (MAC) at RAF Mildenhall in June 1977. The aircraft carries the command shield on its rear fuselage and the badge of the operating wing, the 317th Tactical Airlift Wing, based at Pope AFB, NC, on its forward fuselage. *Martin Horseman*

Right: C-130Es of the 37th Tactical Airlift Squadron on the ramp at Rhein-Main AB, Frankfurt, Germany, in mid-1979. This MAC squadron provides tactical airlift support to US Air Forces in Europe (USAFE). *Martin Horseman*

Left: The Forces Armees Royales, of Morocco, has 20-plus H model Hercules, three of them converted from the transport to the tanker role as KC-130Hs. At least one Herk is known to have been destroyed by a shoulder-launched SAM-7 in Morocco's continuing border dispute against Polisario guerillas in the western Sahara. *Lockheed*

Above: Algeria's Force Arienne Algerienne received six C-130Hs in 1981, paid for the by the United States, as a 'thank you' for that country's role in negotiations towards freeing the American hostages held captive by Iran. The Herks joined a force whose other front-line equipment is largely Soviet-manufactured. *Lockheed*

Right: Abu Dhabi's small air force has four H model Hercules in its inventory. *Lockheed*

54

Above: C-130s of the Fuerza Aerea Argentina were heavily involved in the Falklands war with Britain in the middle of 1982, operating into and out of Port Stanley airfield until just before the British forces recaptured it and, according to some reports, being used as bombers in ineffectual raids against the Royal Navy. Argentina has seven H models and two more configured as tankers in the KC-130H designation. *Lockheed*

Left: The Royal Australian Air Force was the first overseas force to acquire the Hercules, taking the final 12 'As' off the Lockheed production line under provisions of the US Military Assistance Programme, to replace C-47 Dakotas. First deliveries, to No 36 Squadron, were in December 1958. The RAAF then took a further 12 Herks, E versions, in 1966 and later still, 12 'Hs'. Pictured: C-130A (front), C-130E, and C-130H. *Lockheed*

Below left: RAAF C-130Hs over Sydney. *Lockheed*

55

Above: Another NATO operator of the C-130H is the Royal Danish Air Force, whose Hercules-equipped squadron is *Esk 721*. *Lockheed Corporation*

Below: C-130H Hercules of the Belgian Air Force operate with No 20 Squadron at Melsbroek, on the military side of Brussels international airport. *Lockheed Corporation*

Below: A Royal Air Force Hercules C1, XV295, pictured landing at RAF Leuchars in September 1974 — at that time the aircraft was still finished in the 'desert' camouflage scheme adopted to facilitate operations in the Middle East. *Martin Horseman*

Bottom: A memorable line-up of 25 C-130 Hercules at the Hercules Meet which formed part of the International Air Tattoo held at RAF Greenham Common in June 1979. The Meet marked the 25th anniversary of the YC-130 prototype's first flight in August 1954,

and the Silver Jubilee event brought together examples of the Hercules from over the world. Heading the line-up was the very first example of the type to enter service, a USAF C-130A, s/n 55-0023, which was delivered to the 463rd Troop Carrier Wing at Ardmore AFB, Ok, on 9 December 1956 (at the time of the Meet '023' was assigned to the US Air Force Reserve's 928th Tactical Airlift Group). Among the aircraft beyond '023' were an RAF Hercules C1, XV200, and a red and white painted HC-130H of the US Coast Guard from Kodiak, Alaska. *Martin Horseman*

Below: With its own aerospace industry, the Forca Aerea Brasileira, the Brazilian Air Force, is becoming increasingly self-reliant for equipment, but has 16 Hercules on strength, in three versions. Eleven of them are 'Es', and five 'Hs'. Two 'Hs' are in the KC-130 refuelling configuration, and two 'Es' are RC-130 search and rescue aircraft. *Lockheed*

Bottom: Royal Canadian Air Force was an early important customer for the Hercules, and has taken a total of 33 over the years. First four, B versions, were delivered in 1960, but three were resold to Lockheed, and the fourth written off. Then followed 24 'Es', starting in December 1964, with five Es in 1974-75. Following Canadian practice, the Herks were designated CC-130E and CC-130H, and are now operated by the Canadian Armed Forces, into which the Canadian navy, the army and air force were amalgamated in the early 1960s. *Lockheed*

Above: The Colombian Air Force, the Fuerza Aerea Colombiana, acquired three B version Hercules in 1971. These were the aircraft which Canada sold back to Lockheed when it began to receive its E versions. *Lockheed*

Below: Camouflaged Canadian Herk taking off from Nellis AFB on a Red Flag '84 operation. *Frank B. Mormillo*

Bottom: Dubai, as part of the United Arab Emirates, with Abu Dhabi, Amman, Fujairah, Ras al-Khaimah, Sharjah and Umm-al-Qaiwan, supplies one L-100-30 civilian Herk to the UAE Air Force. The UAEAF also has four C-130Hs in its inventory. *Lockheed*

Above: The **RAF** received a total of 66 Hercules C1s, or C-130Ks, which are the UK operated version of the C-130H. This view shows XV292 over a winter landscape in England. *Lockheed Corporation*

Below: The Cameroon Air Force was one of the first customers for the C-130H-30 stretched version of the military Hercules pioneered by the Royal Air Force and Marshalls of Cambridge. The single aircraft ordered by Cameroon in this configuration at the time of writing shows off its distinctive desert paintwork. *Lockheed Corporation*

Above right: First C-130H for the Arab Republic of Egypt Air Force against the classic backdrop of the pyramids. Since then, Egypt has ordered a total of 23 'Hs', all of them for the transport role, except two, which, designated EC-130Hs, are tasked with electronic intelligence gathering. *Lockheed*

Right: The transport wing of the Ecuadorian Air Force, the Fuerza Aerea Ecuatoriana, operates three C-130Hs, alongside Douglas DC-6s, BAe 748s, and DHC-5 Buffalos. The FAE may be a small force, but it has one of the most modern fleets in South America, including Jaguar, Mirage F1s and Northrop Tigers. *Lockheed*

Below: Parachutists climb aboard one of 12 C-130H Hercules in service with the Greek Air Force, Elliniki Aeroporia, all operating in the transport role. *Lockheed*

Above: The Indonesian Air Force, TNI-AU, was an early foreign client of Lockheed for the Herk, introducing 10 'Bs' in 1963, and since adding to the fleet to the extent that there are 28 of various versions in service. In addition to the 'Bs', Indonesia has on strength four 'Hs', seven stretched C-130H-30s, and seven civilianised L-100-30s. *Lockheed*

Below: The Bolivian Air Force took two C-130Hs and a L-100-30 (see p92). Shortly after delivery the first was operating over the Andes out of La Paz — the world's highest civil airport at 13,400ft. *Lockheed*

Below: An RAF Hercules C1K, XV204, at Wideawake airfield, Ascension Island in August 1982. The C1K is an air-to-air refuelling tanker version of the RAF transport, which was rushed into service during the Falklands campaign that year; in addition to extra fuel tankage and the fitting of a hose and drogue refuelling system working from the rear fuselage, the aircraft were equipped with fuel receiving probes, as seen here. *Allan Burney*

Above: Indonesian C-130-MP drops a rescue package on a maritime patrol exercise. Glass observation door, located on either side of the cargo compartment, can be seen under the wing trailing edge. *Lockheed*

Left: Close-up of the Indonesian C-130-MP observation door shows operator with camera. Camera is linked to the aircraft's navigation systems and provides documentary pictures of surface targets, providing precise latitude and longitude, date, and time. *Lockheed*

Above: Kuwait's small air force's inventory includes five Hercules, all civil versions. Pictured here is one of two L-100-20s, and four L-100-30s were scheduled for delivery during 1983. *Lockheed*

Below: Of nine C-130Hs operated by the Royal Malaysian Air Force, six are used as transports, and three as maritime patrollers, designated C-130H-MP. First aircraft went to the fleet in 1975-76. *Lockheed*

Above: The Libyan Air Force operates seven C-130Hs, and has a further eight on order, but these are held under embargo in the United States, adding to the problems of a force which does not have enough transport aircraft for its needs. The air force is largely dependent on Soviet bloc personnel for its operation. *Lockheed*

Left: Aeronautica Militare Italiano, the Italian Air Force, is a longtime user of the Herk, having ordered its 14 H versions in the early 1970s. Italy is an important NATO member, and has allocated 19 of its air force squadrons to that organisation. *Lockheed*

Below left: Royal Jordanian Air Force originally acquired two ex-USAF C-130Bs, and now has four H models in service. *Lockheed*

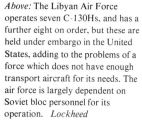

67

Above right: Hercules play a vital role in the Israel Defence Force, and over the years that country has been a strong supporter of the aircraft, with a number of different types passing through its fleet. The IAF originally acquired 12 'Es' and four 'Hs' from 1971 onwards, and in 1972 received a batch of 12 former USAF 'Es'. It now operates around a dozen Herks, mostly in the transport role, but at least two as KC-130H tankers. *Lockheed*

Right: Iran has one of the biggest foreign fleets of Hercules, orders totalling 60 — 28 C-130Es and 32 C-130Hs, all in the transport role. Orders were placed under the regime of the Shah, starting with four 'Bs' delivered as early as 1963 (and later sold to Pakistan) but what the tally is today, with an absence of spares following the revolution, and with the attrition of the war with Iraq, is impossible to say. *Lockheed*

Below: North Yemen's Yemen Arab Republic Air Force bought two C-130Hs as transports, and these fly alongside mainly Soviet-built aviation equipment, including An 26s and 24s. *Lockheed*

Below: South African Air Force has one of the oldest Hercules fleets, its seven C-130Bs, one of which is pictured here, having been in service since 1963. All are used as transports. *Lockheed*

Bottom: Swedish-registered Hercules have been used on international mercy missions abroad, as well as with the armed forces. First C-130, an ex-USAF aircraft, was leased from Lockheed, and then bought in March, 1963. Flygvapen, the Swedish Air Force, now has eight Herks, two E models, and six Hs, one of which is pictured. *Lockheed*

Above: Chilean Air Force, the Fuerza Aerea de Chile, has two transport C-130Hs is service. They were delivered in the early 1970s. *Lockheed*

Below: Turk Hava Kuvvetleri, the Turkish Air Force, was one of the earliest customers from abroad for the Hercules, acquiring eight 'Es' in the 1960s. It still operates at least seven of these. *Lockheed*

7
Service with the RAF

The Royal Air Force became a major user of the Hercules as a result of a decision taken by the British Government early in 1965 to buy a total of 66 following cancellation of a project for its own short take-off and landing freighter, the HS681. Britain at that time badly needed a replacement for its ageing Hastings and Beverley transports, and chose the C-130H version of the Hercules, although insisting on numerous changes in the specification of the basic design.

Among the main changes which were demanded were, the use of British avionics equipment instead of the standard US fit, including radar, radio and autopilot, and British roller equipment and lashings within the fuselage. Although the decision to purchase

Below: In a push for world sales of the stretched dash 30 model to world air forces, Lockheed indulged in a little ballyhoo at the 1982 Farnborough air show. *Lockheed*

Hercules was taken in London in February 1965, the first batch of 24 was not actually ordered until June of that year. A further 24 were ordered in October that same year, and a final batch of 18 in March the following year.

As part of the deal, Lockheed had to place sub-contract work in Britain, and Scottish Aviation was selected, after tenders from a number of different companies, to produce external fuel tank pylons, undercarriage frames, and top and side fuselage skin panels, representing about 2% of the total work on each aircraft. Scottish Aviation (now British Aerospace) completed the contract so successfully at its Prestwick, Scotland, works that it won numerous others to produce similar items for Hercules. Two other companies benefited from British Government insistence on 'Anglicising' the Herks for the RAF — Marshall, of Cambridge, being responsible for the painting of the aircraft after they had been delivered, customer support, modifications, and trial installations, and Marston-Excelsior, for the radomes.

The first Hercules for the RAF, designated C-130K in the US, and C Mk 1 by the RAF, flew at Marietta on 19 October 1966, and the second, which was to be the first to be handed over to Britain, on 16 December. Wearing RAF roundels, but otherwise unpainted, the first aircraft was flown to Britain, and after a spell at Marshall's, was officially accepted by the Service on 25 April 1967. An initial 26 crews were trained by the United States Air Force, and RAF crew training began at Thorney Island, Hants, by 242 OCU in June 1967.

No 36 became the first RAF squadron to receive Hercules, whose roles in the Service were to carry up to 62 paratroops, 92 troops, 74 stretchers in the aeromedical evacuation role, four pallets each carrying 8,000lb, two carrying 16,000lb, or one with 30,000lb. RAF Hercules were also earmarked to carry scout

Above: The Royal Air Force acquired 66 Hercules in a decision taken by the British Government in 1965. The RAF version was based on the C-130H model, but had a number of changes in the basic design, with much of the equipment and some of the sub-assembly work coming from Britain. Herks should be in service with the RAF until well into the 1990s. *RAF*

Right: Paratroops wait to go on board an RAF Hercules through the doors at either side of the aircraft through which they will later jump. The C1 carries up to 62 paratroops, the stretched C3 up to 92. *RAF*

Below right: Whirling prop blades of an RAF Hercules kick up a dust storm as it taxies down the sort of unprepared strip for which it was designed, and which makes it a popular packhorse for so many air forces. *RAF*

cars, Land Rovers, helicopters, and armoured cars, and were later cleared to drop supplies in the British version of LAPES from as low as 20ft.

The RAF's first squadron, based at Lyneham, Wilts, completed its re-equipment with the new aircraft by September 1967, and shortly afterwards No 48 Squadron, then based at RAF Changi, Singapore, began to be re-equipped, deliveries ending in the middle of the following year. Other RAF squadrons to receive Hercules were Nos 70 (which was based at Akrotiri, Cyprus, as part of the Near East Air Force), 24, 30 and 47. Nos 36 and 48 were later disbanded, and the remainder, together with the OCU, are now based at Lyneham. Two squadrons were for a time based at RAF Fairford, Glos.

Hercules took part in the British withdrawal from Aden in November 1967, as their first big operation, flying 2,150 passengers and 108 tons of assorted cargo on 52 flights totalling 255 hours between Khormaksar, and RAF Muharraq, Bahrain. Although the aircraft were new in service, and crew experience was limited, the operation was a complete success, with turnround times in Aden of half an hour maximum, and only a single late departure.

The RAF's fleet of Hercules has since then been involved in numerous mercy missions throughout the world (mention of which is made in other chapters) and military operations, including the ferrying of over 7,000 people during fighting in Cyprus between the sovereign bases of Akrotiri and Dhekelia. A total of 139 passengers travelled on one flight. RAF Hercules also provided logistics support for the team which supervised elections in Rhodesia, during which one aircraft collected a bullet hole in the fuselage near the co-pilot's seat, the shot coming from an unknown source, and also for the RAF aerobatic team, the Red Arrows.

But the fleet's 'finest hour' was, without doubt, the Falklands war, in the summer of 1982, during which they provided logistics support for the British forces which recaptured this British territory lying on the edge of Antarctica. Without them, it is extremely

Below: RAF Herk No 218, a C1, drops a stores package out of its rear cargo ramp door. Drops such as this were invaluable during the Falklands campaign for replenishing supplies of the task force before the Port Stanley runway was recaptured. *RAF*

Above: Mix of unstretched C1s and stretched C3s on the apron at the RAF Hercules base at Lyneham. Picture was evidently taken before the Falklands crisis, as none of the C1s have refuelling probes fitted. *RAF*

Right: Locking of horns: two RAF C1s, Nos 298 and 185, point their refuelling probes — specially fitted in a rush job for the Falklands crisis — at each other in the RAF Lyneham workshops. *Author*

Above: Big windows on the Hercules flight deck give excellent vision for refuelling hook-up with Victor K2 tanker. *RAF*

doubtful whether the campaign could have been carried out.

In the initial stages of the campaign, in April, Hercules were used to fly stores for the naval task force, which was to sail to the Falklands, to Wideawake air base, on Ascension Island. They also carried medical stores and personnel to Gibraltar to join the liner Uganda, converted into a hospital ship for the period of the campaign. To increase the Hercules' duration, engineers at Lyneham fitted auxiliary tanks in the forward cabins of some, but it soon became obvious that if the aircraft were to back up the fleet as it steamed farther and farther south, and then to support operations actually in the Falklands, an in-flight refuelling capability was essential.

As Operation 'Corporate', as the Falklands campaign was called, rolled on in April, Marshall's was tasked with the rush job of making that capability a reality. At short notice, the company adapted refuelling probes, originally designed for Vulcans, fitting the first within the space of 10 days, after which it was delivered to the Government research establishment at Boscombe Down, Wilts, for testing. A total of 16 Hercules, all C Mk 1s (stretching of RAF Hercules into the C Mk 3 version is described later) were con-

verted, and are now known as PLR2s. Other modifications to these aircraft were, installation of floodlights positioned to light the probe from the right-hand windows of the flight deck, a refuelling control panel above the navigator's station, and Omega as an additional navigation aid.

Marshall's was also tasked with converting four C Mk 1s to the tanker role, and in a further rush job hose reel units were installed on the cargo ramp, with deployment through the ramp door. External lighting standard for tanker aircraft was fitted, as was the Omega navaid, and the aircraft were themselves fitted with probes so that they could take on fuel in flight if necessary. Test couplings were made from Boscombe Down with a succession of different aircraft, including Harriers, Nimrods, Phantoms, and other Hercules, and after minor problems had been solved, all four aircraft, designated C Mk 1 (K), were delivered to the RAF within three months of the initial request.

Crews from the Lyneham base then became heavily engaged in refuelling training, one problem being that the Victors from which the Hercules took fuel on the South Atlantic route could fly no slower than 230kts, while top speed of the Herks was 210kts. To overcome this discrepancy, the 'toboggan' routine was evolved, in which both aircraft descended at a rate of about 500ft/min, so that the Hercules' speed was between 230 and 240kts, similar to that of the tanker.

First long-range flight by a Hercules into the total exclusion zone around the Falklands using in-flight refuelling was made on 16 May 1982, when stores and parachutists were dropped to a Royal Navy ship. This flight lasted 24hr 5min, and covered 6,300nm, but as the British landings took place, and the need for further supplies became intense, such operations became virtually routine. By the beginning of June, the Hercules fleet had flown the equivalent of 3million miles in the air, or 10,000 flight hours. Port Stanley airfield was recaptured, but remained unusable due to damage, and round trips with refuelling of 26 hours from Ascension occurred frequently (Lyneham has a 24-hour club, with a large membership, of aircrew who suffered the noisy environment of a Herk for that

period or longer during the Falklands campaign). An extra pilot and navigator was added to the normal crew of four on flights expected to last more than 20 hours.

Ironically, the last flight by the Argentinian Air Force out of Port Stanley on 13 June, as the British closed in had been by a Hercules. The first RAF Hercules to land there came in 11 days later. It carried an air movement unit whose task was to load and unload aircraft, and a day later the first Hercules carrying an operational payload touched down. Its complement of passengers included the former Governor of the Falklands, Rex Hunt, returning from London.

With Port Stanley opened as an RAF base, the strain on the Hercules and their crews was lessened significantly, although 13-hour sectors from Ascension remained normal. On a number of occasions it was necessary for aircraft to return to Ascension without landing on the Falklands because of sudden changes in weather over the islands. A few emergency diversions were also made to Brazil. During a period in the summer of 1982 when the Port Stanley airfield was shut while extensions and improvements were being made, the Hercules again carried out round trips from Ascension, dropping supplies by parachute, and picking up mail by air snatch.

At the time of writing, the massive airlift to support the British Services on the Falklands by way of Ascension Island continues, and the Hercules continue to play their important part. After the ceasefire, the RAF described the operation by its transport and supply personnel as, 'one of their biggest battles since the 1940s', and by that time, over 500 supply sorties had

Below: RAF C1 No 179 holds, at the time of writing, the world record for nonstop flights by Hercules — 28hr 3min to the Falklands and back from Ascension. Aircraft was commanded by Flt Lt Terry Locke, of No 70 Squadron. Headwinds encountered in each direction during a sortie to drop stores to a Rapier battery accounted for the long duration. *Author*

been flown by the Herks and VC10s, backed up by a small number of flights by civil 707s and Belfasts. Total flying time of this fleet, mostly by the Hercules, exceeded 15,000 hours, and involved the carriage of over 7,000 tons of freight, including 114 vehicles, 22 helicopters, and nearly 6,000 troops and support personnel.

The operation on Ascension was masterminded by the Tactical Supply Wing from RAF Stafford, which was linked by way of satellite with the Supply Control Centre at RAF Hendon and, through this, was able to exploit operationally a system of inventory control unique among the armed forces of the world. The suppliers in Ascension were able to maintain constant touch with those responsible for organising the massive loading and transport of stores by air. No fewer than 38 ships were supplied in this way through Ascension in the first six weeks of the conflict.

The whole enormous operation was made more difficult by the immense distances involved, by the highly-unpredictable weather met en route, and particularly in the Ascension-Falklands sector, and by the fact that a refuelling capability had to be rushed through, which meant that many of the crews had little experience of this exact form of flying. A Hercules crew member recalled the experience: 'In the days when because of the task force operation we were operating in radio silence, it was always an immense feeling of relief to see that other aircraft, even though to refuel it had to come closer than our instincts told us was safe.'

'The refuelling operations were tricky, and for 20 minutes or so you used to sweat a little. But it was more tense in the fighting zone, because the Hercules

Above: Herk No 205, a C1 with probe, was the aircraft which carried the Prime Minister, Mrs Margaret Thatcher, from Ascension to the Falklands. The aircraft developed an engine fault before departure on the return journey, and the PM was transferred to No 179. *Author*

Left: Pictured in the RAF Lyneham cargo shed after being unloaded is the Wonderland caravan which provided a semi-soundproof haven for Mrs Thatcher on her flight from Ascension to the Falklands inside Herk No 205. The caravan, equipped with comfortable seating and the usual facilities, was wheeled into the aircraft's cargo compartment and connected up to its services. *Author*

flew completely without defences. Frankly, our worry was the chance we might get shot down by our own ships or by our Harriers. Remember, the Argentines were flying Hercules, too, and they did try to bomb shipping.'

In January 1983, when Mrs Thatcher paid an official visit to the Falklands with her husband Denis, the Prime Minister travelled by Herk. Her journey began from RAF Brize Norton by RAF VC10, in which she was flown to Ascension. There she transferred to RAF Hercules No 205, a special caravan

having been run up the rear ramp and installed in the fuselage for her use. In it were comfortable seats, table and a toilet, and Mr and Mrs Thatcher were thus able to pass the 13-hour journey in a slightly higher standard of comfort, and with a lot less noise, than most Hercules passengers. The aircraft was refuelled three times between Ascension and Port Stanley, and on arrival the PM described the flight as, 'most comfortable'. It was planned that the party should return in the same aircraft, with its caravan still installed, but at the last moment, 205 developed engine trouble, and

Right: The plan view of the C3 which took part in the flying display at the 1982 Farnborough air show, shows graphically the length of the fuselage in comparison to the C1. Extra length is achieved by inserting a 100in plug ahead of the wing, and an 80in plug aft. *Brian M. Service*

Below: A total of 30 of the original RAF purchase of 66 C1s is eventually to be 'stretched' by Marshall's, of Cambridge, to the longer C3 version (seen here — right — flying behind a C1). The stretch gives a 40% increase in freight volume, but no degradation of the STOL performance into rough strips. Following RAF pioneering of the longer Herk, three other countries, Algeria, Cameroon and Indonesia quickly ordered it for their air forces. *Lockheed*

No 179 carried the VIPs in normal Herk passenger conditions, there not being time for the caravan to be transferred.

Although there are four Hercules squadrons and the OCU at Lyneham, the aircraft operate in a pool, and do not wear squadron badges. Only Mk 1 (unstretched) aircraft were converted for inflight refuelling, and this conversion tended to split the force into two sections, with Nos 24 and 30 Squadrons concentrating on tanker operations, and 47 and 70 on the tactical role. At the time of writing, the plan was to stretch 30 RAF Hercules into the Mk 3 version, and the first, aircraft No 223, was re-delivered by Lockheed at Marietta, Georgia, in December 1979, with subsequent aircraft being modified by Marshall's. The stretch is carried out by inserting a 100in 'plug' in the fuselage in front of the wing, and an 80in plug aft of the wing to increase the aircraft's cargo compartment length from 40.4ft to 55.4ft, which permits the loading of two additional cargo pallets. Or the Mk 3 can carry 128 fully equipped troops, instead of 92 on the Mk 1, or 98 litter patients and three attendants, instead of 74 patients and two attendants. Operating weight is 77,553lb, and maximum payload 39,799lb. In its stretched form, the Hercules retains the same short take-off and landing performance on rough strips as the Mk 1, and aircrew say that it is very difficult to detect any difference in the flight characteristics of the two versions.

The RAF Mk 2 version of the Hercules consists of one aircraft only, taken from the original buy of 66, and extensively modified by Marshall's for the RAF Meteorological Research Flight, on whose behalf it operates out of the Royal Aircraft Establishment, Farnborough, Hants. Perhaps the most distinctive-looking Hercules of them all, the Mk 2 has its characteristic radar nose removed and replaced by a boom, some 26ft long. This has installed in it a pitot head, yaw and pitch detectors, and temperature sensors; the reason for the inordinate length of the boom is to place these sensitive instruments far ahead of the aircraft, and so out of the disturbance which it causes to the air around it in flight. The removed radar was placed in a large pod standing on a pylon over the roof of the flight deck, so producing a further easily-identified feature. Underwing pods carry weather-measuring instruments.

Marshall's also carried out an extensive redesign job on the interior of the Mk 2 so that it could fly scientists and their equipment. An installation at the rear of the Hercules enables radio sondes to be shot from the aircraft without any loss in pressure in the fuselage. There are positions for two operators of this equipment, and racks to hold 60 sondes. The scientists work during flight in a special van wheeled on board, in the same way as was the caravan, mentioned earlier, which conveyed Mrs Thatcher to the Falklands, but for take-off and landing they are accommodated in 15 seats facing to the rear. An extra seat was placed on the flight deck for the project officer. The Mk 2 was given a maximum mission time with two standard additional fuel tanks, one under each wing, and has been to many parts of the world in pursuit of weather data. In 1975, for instance, the aircraft was based in Senegal as part of an international programme to investigate tropical weather conditions over the Atlantic Ocean.

Below: Perhaps the most distinctive Hercules of them all was the British W Mk 2. A converted RAF C1, based on the C-130H, it was modified by Marshall's of Cambridge for weather reconnaissance, stationed at the Royal Aircraft Establishment, Farnborough, England. The modifications included the 22ft long nose probe, which entailed moving the radar antenna to the pod on top of the flight deck. *RAE*

Above: RAF C1 does a quick wheels-up after taking off at the 1979 Greenham Common air tattoo, which celebrated the 25th anniversary of the Hercules' maiden flight. In the background is the line up of the Herks which flew in for this occasion. *Brian M. Service*

Right: Loaded for LAPES; a Land Rover in its special cradle, with parachutes packed at the rear, on which it will be pulled from the RAF Hercules in a low altitude parachute extraction exercise. *RAF*

Below right: A truck is waved away from the rear ramp of RAF Herk 189 after unloading stores into its cavernous interior. *Author*

The capacious interior and carrying capacity of the Hercules is well illustrated here as one of two Scout helicopters carried from the UK is unloaded at Kai Tak airport, Hong Kong. The Scouts were sent to the colony to reinforce the garrison in its attempts to halt illegal immigration from China and Vietnam. *MoD (both)*

Above: RAF Hercules No 306 stands on ground power at Lyneham. The base has four Herk squadrons, Nos 24, 30, 47 and 70, and the OCU, but the aircraft are in pool, and wear no squadron crests. *Author*

Right: Work in progress inside a Lyneham maintenance hangar on a Hercules engine. Props have been switched to coarse pitch for the occasion. *Author*

Below: RAF mechanics service one of a Herk's Allison turboprops in the open on a cold and blowy day at RAF Lyneham. *Author*

Above left: The Hercules' main undercarriage wheels are usually hidden away, but here, during maintenance, are fully exposed. Fat tyres were designed for landings on soft surfaces, and the front wheel ploughs a hard surface for that at the rear. *Author*

Above: Bird's eye view of one of the RAF's Hercules was taken from on top of the wing. The walkway along the fuselage is clearly defined and the escape hatch through which this vertiginous photographic exercise was approached can be seen on the port side of the fin. *Author*

Left: It is possible to see how the Hercules gained one of its nicknames — Fat Albert — from this head-on view of the endurance champion, RAF Mk 1 No 179. Probes, fitted only to unstretched Mk 1 aircraft, were originally designed for Vulcans. *Author*

8
In Civilian Guise

Lockheed offered the Hercules in its civilian guise in two main versions, the L-100-20, which is 100in longer than the standard military C-130, and the L-100-30, which is 180in longer. The stretches enable the Herks to carry up to 33% more cargo, but the aircraft retain the original aircraft's ability to operate into and out of difficult sites, including runways made of sand and gravel, or on frozen lakes. A James Bay Energy Corporation L-100-20, flown by Quebecair pilots, made what is believed to be the southernmost ice landing when, in February 1974, a Hercules

Below: The L-100-30 prototype on a test flight, with the 'plugs' in the fuselage, which lengthened the aircraft 6ft 8½in over the dash 20, clearly visible. The stretch enabled Saturn Airways to carry a full set of three Rolls-Royce RB211 engines from Britain to Palmdale, California, for the Lockheed TriStar wide-bodied airliner. *Lockheed*

touched down on ice 42in thick forming a landing strip 4,500ft long at LaGran 3, a construction site at the St James Bay oilfield at the northwest of Montreal.

To 'stretch' the Hercules into the civilian version, Lockheed insert plugs in the fuselage both fore and aft of the wing. An original version, the L-100, carried six standard containers or pallets in its interior, while the dash 20 carried seven and the dash 30 eight. All of the L-100s have now been converted to the larger standard. The first stretched commercial C-130 was the demonstrator One World Hercules, a dash 20, which was developed from a C-130E, and certificated by the US Federal Aviation Administration to fly as a civilian freighter. In a concentrated sale effort, the aircraft was flown around the world by a crew headed by Joe Garrett, Lockheed-Georgia's chief production pilot. Making its maiden flight, the Hercules remained aloft for 25hr 1min, and operated for all but 36 minutes of that time on only two of its four engines. This then record flight was made at a loitering speed of between 130mph and 140mph (compared with the Hercules's normal cruising speed of 360mph).

The demonstrator L-383B was the first commercial Hercules to go to work in Alaska, where it was leased to Alaska Airlines, in 1965. In the space of 20 days, it proved its usefulness by hauling 3½million pounds of heavy oil-drilling equipment between Fairbanks, and a remote drilling site on the frozen tundra near the Arctic Ocean. Roller conveyors installed on the floor of the fuselage speeded up the loading and unloading of the equipment, which included an enormous mud pump, caterpillar tractors weighing 45,000lb each, fuel storage tanks, sleeping trailers, and barrels of diesel fuel.

As a result of this demonstration, civilian Herks came to stay in Alaska, and played a vital part in the great oil rush which opened up the territory. In 1974, at the height of the construction of the Alaska pipeline,

which was to bring the newly found oil out of this inhospitable territory, Alaska Airlines employed six of the aircraft and hauled one million pounds of goods each day. During that same year, the AA Herks transported, it is reckoned, 22million gallons of diesel fuel to distant points all over Alaska, including 14million gallons to pipeline camps, and created 'instant towns' along the route of the pipeline by bringing in 1,200 portable cabins from Anchorage and Fairbanks.

Average daily utilisation for the Hercules was 12 hours, but 17 were logged by one of them, on 12 March 1974. At this time, the airline had 28

Hercules crews on its payroll, each consisting of a captain, co-pilot, flight engineer, and a loadmaster. In addition to oil-related equipment, the aircraft hauled a wide variety of loads — trees, prefabricated post offices, and fresh fish destined for canneries.

Word of the efficiency of the new freighter spread to civil airlines, and by the middle 1970s 10 carriers around the world were flying 60 or more of them on an amazing diversity of tasks. When the British ocean liner the *Queen Elizabeth II* was stranded in New York with a disabled engine, a TIA Hercules flew to Britain and brought back a replacement part weighing

Above: L-100-20 prototype comes together in the Lockheed shops. The original L-100 company demonstrator made its maiden flight on 20 April 1964 and was later modified to a dash 200, in which version it carried the colours of several airlines. On the maiden flight, the first civil Herk, named *One World Hercules*, stayed in the air for 25hr 1min, flying most of that time on only two of its four engines. *Lockheed*

Below: Stretching of the L-100-20 airframe into the 'Super Stretch' dash 30 in progress at Lockheed's Marietta, Georgia, works. The dash 30 carries eight large pallets and offers 4,700cu ft of space for this type of cargo — compared with the standard Hercules, which takes six pallents. *Lockheed*

Right: The L-110-30 offers airlines and other operators 50,000lb payload, but still has the short take-off and landing performance into remote strips of earlier, smaller versions. Seen here in the colours of Canadian operator Northwest Territorial Airways. *Lockheed*

Below right: James Bay Energy Corp L-100-20 parks on the edge of a muddy oil field in northern Canada. Flown by Quebecair pilots, a Hercules of this operator made the southernmost landing on ice, at an oil prospecting site at St James Bay, north of Montreal. *Lockheed*

45,000lb — and had it in New York within 11 hours after the order had been received. TIA also flew a complete base camp, weighing 900 tons in all, deep into the jungle in Guatemala, its Hercules landing on an airstrip cut out of the virgin forest. And TIA also flew a turbine from its manufacturers in Ohio, USA, to a remote pipeline site in Alaska to replace one which had been closed down by an explosion. The unit weighed 45,000lb.

It was TIA whose aircraft became the first to beat the 30,000 hours-in-the-air record. The aircraft was originally delivered by Lockheed to Delta Air Lines in 1966, and Delta had it stretched 8.3ft to dash 20 configuration two years later. The aircraft was subsequently acquired by Saturn Airways, which had it stretched again to dash 30, or Super Hercules, configuration. The aircraft became TIA in 1976 when Saturn and Trans International merged, and the record was broken the following year.

After the early days of the civilian Herks, when almost all the loads were hefty items to oilfields, a lucrative trade using the aircraft started up carrying high-priority freight, such as perishable fruit, fashion goods, and livestock. Alaska International transported a whale weighing 9,000lb and measuring 21.4ft in length to a wild-life park in Japan, picking it up in

Tokyo after it had been flown across the Pacific from San Francisco in a Boeing 747. Saturn carried an entire television station to China to give live coverage of President Nixon's visit to that country.

But hopes by Lockheed of further developments of the Hercules were never realised. Among new versions promoted by the company were, bigger bodies, with more-powerful, more-efficient engines and propellers, including a 'double-bubble' fuselage design which was to have a gross weight of 191,000lb, and a payload of 62,000lb and, specifically for the civil market, the L-100-50 and -60, with longer bodies, the L-100-31 and L-100-30C, respectively all-passenger and passenger/cargo, and a twin-engined version, the L-400. Plans for such developments ground to a halt as aerospace money became tight all over the world, operators indicated that they were well-satisfied with existing versions of the Hercules, continuing to order them in numbers, and as a new generation of wide-bodied jet airliners with large belly holds began to carry some of the international air freight which had in the past gravitated towards the C-130.

Over 70 civil versions of the Hercules have so far been ordered by operators, both airlines and government agencies around the world, and many of them have changed hands at a later stage. Transamerica had

Right: SCIBE, of Zaire, operated one L-100-30, alongside the seven C-130H Herks of the Zaire Government. *Lockheed*

Below: One of two of the original L-100s acquired by Pakistan International Airlines sits in a highly-polished state on the apron. *Lockheed*

Right: Southern Air Transport, based in Miami, Florida, acquired two L-100-20s, one of which is seen here being prepared to load palletised freight. *Lockheed*

one of the largest fleets, and at one time was flying 50% of all United States cargo transported by supplemental airlines. An executive of the company gave the reasoning behind the choice of aircraft: 'When the fuel crisis came, we looked at fuel consumption of the big jets, and how much fuel the Hercules, and its sister aircraft, the Lockheed Electra, burned. The jets burn 2,500gal an hour, compared with the 750gal an hour of the prop-jets. And so we decreased operations with the jets, and gave more fuel to the turbo-props.'

Left: Just an everyday landing field for the Hercules, seen through a C-130 flight-deck window, as an L-100 of one of the civil operators is on approach. The strip is at Dietrich, in the Alaskan oil field. *Lockheed*

Below left: On a snow-covered field somewhere north of the Arctic Circle, a Herk delivers a load of mixed essentials to keep an outlying outpost of industry going for a few more days. *Lockheed*

Above: A civil Herk poses against a backcloth of the sort of terrain, jagged mountains covered with snow, in which it has proved itself over the years, and where the crews of other transports of its size would hesitate to go. *Lockheed*

Below: Pacific Western Airlines, of Calgary, Canada, has been a longtime user of the civilian Hercules, and operates both the dash 20 and 30. Owned by the Government of Alberta, the airline flies scheduled services throughout the North-West of Canada and, with its Herks, world-wide cargo operations. *Lockheed*

Left: West German airline Wirtschaftsflug Rhein-Main bought one L-100-30 in 1981 for world-wide cargo charter operations. The aircraft is seen here on a fly-by at Lockheed's Marietta plant before being delivered. *Lockheed*

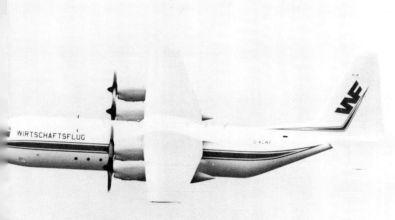

89

Right: PEMEX, the Mexican carrier, ordered one L-100-30. The aircraft was widely used in connection with oil-exploration work. *Lockheed*

Below: Following the discovery of oil in Alaska in 1967, Alaska International Air switched roles from light charter to heavylift, and standardised on the Herk. At the most recent count, the airline had five L-100-30s one of which is seen here in typical inhospitable Alaskan territory. In service with AIA and other operators, the civilian Hercules has played a major and vital role in opening up the Alaskan oilfields. *Lockheed*

Below: The L-100-20 demonstrator is the subject of considerable interest during a stop at a remote spot during a demonstration and sales tour. *Lockheed*

Bottom: Linhas Aereas de Angola is another African operator of the civil Herk. The airline operates an extensive network of scheduled services both within the country and to international destinations. *Lockheed*

Above: Safair Freighters, formed in 1969 as a subsidiary of Safmarine to operate cargo charter flights, may claim to have been the world's biggest operator of the civilian Herk, having originally acquired 17. At the time of writing, it had 11 dash 30s and one dash 20. From its main base at Jan Smuts airport, it operates Hercules on a daily service for South African Airways between Johannesburg-Durban-Port Elizabeth. *Lockheed*

Right: The government of the Philippines acquired four L-100-20s from the US carrier Flying W, and among these aircraft was the original civil demonstrator. Aircraft link that country's 7,100 islands, carrying out a multitude of tasks, from carrying bulldozers to rice seedlings. The Philippine Herks have also flown to London to collect new currency for the nation. *Lockheed*

Below right: Bolivia acquired two C-130H versions Hercules, and this L-100-30, which is seen in the livery of Transporte Aereo Boliviano. Hercules provide an essential link in a mountainous country, completing journeys with heavy equipment in minutes which would take days by surface transport. *Lockheed*

Left: Transamerica, which took over Saturn Airways in 1976, has a fleet of 12 dash 30 civilian Herks, one of which is pictured loading a freight igloo. The airline was the first Herk operator to beat the 30,000 flying hours record, the aircraft in question being ex-Delta Air Lines. *Lockheed*

Below: Echo Bay Mines' single L-100-20 makes a sprightly take-off from a snow-covered strip at Port Radium. The aircraft was used to carry fuel in its internal tanks for offloading at the Arctic Line mining camps to provide heat for buildings and to generate electricity. *Lockheed*

Above: Pacific Western's handsome L-100-20, in dark blue and white, with an orange and light blue tail insignia, shows that the Herk can shed its drab workaday appearance when tricked out in smart civilian paint. *Lockheed*

Right: Against a typical Middle Eastern setting of sand dunes and palm trees, a Southern Air L-100-20 makes an approach to a landing on a desert strip. *Lockheed*

Below: L-100-30 in the livery of Air Botswana. The airline was formed in 1972, is owned by the Botswana Development Corporation, and flies scheduled passenger and cargo services from Gaborone to Johannesburg and other points in southern Africa. *Lockheed*

9
On Missions of Mercy

Warlike in Vietnam, and in various other theatres of conflict, the Hercules has also built up a reputation over the years as an angel of mercy, flying relief programmes for governments and international agencies throughout the world with a vast miscellany of equipment and specialists, from water purifiers to electrical generators, from drugs and bandages to portable shelters, from doctors to engineers. Earthquakes to famines, typhoons and tidal waves, they have all been the same to the C-130s, whose crews, wearing the insignia of many nations, flew into and out of strips which would have been impossible for any other aircraft of its size and carrying capability, so saving lives which would have otherwise been in jeopardy.

In Chile, in 1960, for instance, Tactical Air Command USAF Herks delivered emergency supplies after the country had been struck by a series of tidal waves, and in the same year, the Hercules were in Alaska, 450 miles north of Point Barrow, where,

equipped with ski landing gear, they rescued scientists when an ice island on which they had been working began to disintegrate.

At about that same period, Hercules carried supplies in to French Equatorial Africa for Dr Alfred Schweitzer's mission, and iron lungs and chest respirators were rushed to Hokkaido, Japan, after the area had been affected by a bad outbreak of poliomyelitis. During the upheaval in the Congo, from 1964 to 1967, Hercules delivered an estimated 150 tons of relief supplies, and flew out with around 12,000 evacuees.

The Dominican republic crisis of 1965 saw the Hercules of the 463rd Troop Carrier Wing from Langley AFB, and the 464th TCW, from Pope AFB, delivering over 16,000 tons of medical and other equipment, including a 100-bed hospital, and taking out some 1,000 refugees. The following year, C-130s were hard at work again in Africa, where they delivered 18 tons of cholera vaccine, in Peru, where they delivered a sawmill weighing around 15tons, and 400 tons of road and bridge-building equipment, in the Dominican Republic (the complete components for a bridge), and in Guatemala (a consignment of iron lungs).

Also in 1965, Hercules from the USAF based in Europe flew 500 tons of food to famine-hit areas of the African state of Chad, and evacuated over 5,000 people from Jordan and Libya during international incidents. Around 55 tons of supplies were flown into

Below: The USAF airlifts food and medicine to Honduras in yet another mercy operation with its Hercules. The ease of unloading is obvious, with the truck backed right up to the cargo floor. *Lockheed*

Peru during that year after that country had been struck by earthquakes, and 25 tons of evaporated milk were poured into Ghana.

Not all of the Hercules rescue missions have been abroad, however. In 1967, for instance, the USAF's workhorses were summoned to the southwestern USA after hurricane Beulah had struck. They delivered 200,000 sandbags to Harlingen, Texan, where floods threatened, and later that same year flew 50,000lb of clothing and food to Arizona for the relief of Navaho Indians whose reservation had been devastated by blizzards.

Italy was the scene of Hercules mercy missions in 1968 when that country was struck by a series of earthquakes, 18 tons of food arriving out of the skies in the capacious holds of the C-130s, but the effort was tiny compared with that which took place in Japan later that same year after a typhoon had passed through — 350 tons being flown in.

Back in the United States in 1969, Hercules from units all over the country were pressed into service to hurry relief supplies into Missouri following depradations by Hurricane Camille. Shortly afterwards, the Herks were off to Chad again, putting down a relief team consisting of 46 assorted personnel and 164 tons of food.

The year 1970 saw Peru again struck by big earthquakes, and the Hercules in action there once more. On this occasion, the damage was so intense that even the C-130s were unable to land on the devastated airstrips, and had to parachute their life-saving supplies. But the local inhabitants later improved the strips to the extent where the Herks could touch down and

take-off again, and by the end of the emergency a rough count showed that 658 tons of food had been flown in in 167 missions out of bases in the Panama Canal zone, while some 1,600 passengers had been conveyed to and from the devastated area.

Hercules donned the colours of the International Red Cross during a relief effort to Jordan following an outbreak of hostilities there. They delivered over 2,000 tons of equipment and supplies, and carried over 1,700 people, in 485 sorties, and at the end left behind some $450,000 worth of supplies given for international development by the Red Cross.

Hercules of the Belgian Air Force acted on behalf of the Red Cross, both Canadian and Swedish, in the Congo in 1960 and 1965, taking food and medical supplies in, and women and children out. USAF Hercules carried Belgian paratroopers into Stanleyville where civilians were being massacred by 'Simba' guerillas, and in a daring operation, often under heavy ground fire, brought 'plane-loads of terrified people to safety. At the end of the operation, King Baudouin presented crews with medals, and said; 'The courage and determination which you have shown have gone right to the heart of our nation. In the space of a few days, you have averted a dreadful fate for 2,000 compatriots and friends. I salute with gratitude the crews of the US Air Force who, by their airmanship and self-control, have carried out this vast operation of transport.'

In the spring of 1973, it was the turn of the Hercules of the Royal Air Force to be involved in a massive international relief operation. The place was the kingdom of Nepal, high in the Himalayas, between

Right: Force Aerienne Belge, the Belgian Air Force, began to introduce the Hercules into its inventory in late 1972, and now has 12 'Hs' operating in the transport mode. *Lockheed*

Above: RAF Hercules were involved in famine relief in Nepal in 1977, delivering 2,000 tons of food to help feed 1.5million starving people in this mountainous kingdom. Here a C1 is about to drop from 50ft a one-ton load of grain in 87lb sacks lashed to plywood pallets. *Lockheed*

Right: Nepalese villagers sift grain brought to them by RAF Herks during the 1977 famine-relief operation. *Lockheed*

India and China, and the cause a bad famine, produced by the failure of harvests following torrential hail, followed closely by drought.

Sufficient grain to avert the disaster was donated by world relief agencies, but in such a mountainous country, the only way of distributing it in time was by air — and this was where the RAF Hercules came into their own. Four million pounds of grain was to be distributed to 1½million population — this was the measure of the task. In response to a call from the Nepalese Government, the British Government soon had 14 aircraft, each loaded with vehicles and other equipment, and 220 men, on the scene, with four aircraft detailed to take part in the relief-dropping exercise.

Supply-dropping was necessary, because there was only one landing site in the area, which embraced six of the highest mountains in the world, all of them over 26,000ft, including the highest, Mount Everest, 29,028ft. Jinking through narrow valleys high up in these mountains, often facing gale-force winds funnelled down them, the RAF Herks shifted 2,000 tons of food in a total of 187 sorties into 10 isolated centres. The exercise was completed in five weeks, which was three weeks ahead of schedule, and well ahead of the monsoon season, which would have made all flying operations in the region impossible. In the words of Mr T. J. O'Brien, the British ambassador to Katmandu, when it was all over; 'The RAF plucked these people from the brink of despair.'

Other mercy missions in which the Hercules of the RAF have been involved over the years have included those into Jordan in 1970, when the aircraft carried hospitals, food, medicines and trucks, and in 1971 into what was East Pakistan (now Bangladesh) from where 480 women and children were evacuated during a ceasefire lasting only 4$\frac{1}{2}$ hours. Royal Norwegian Air Force Hercules were in on a relief operation in the Republic of Yemen in 1970 following a severe drought and, in the same year, carried a surgical unit into Peru following the bad earthquake there. French and Canadian air forces also employed their Hercules during this period to evacuate civilians from the stricken Peruvian areas.

The list of relief missions flown by Hercules of many of the world governments and agencies is too long to detail. Iran, 1978: the town of Tabas, in the Iranian Davir desert, was desolated by a severe earthquake, with the loss of more than 20,000 lives. The Imperial Iranian Air Force sent 12 Hercules and a battalion of troops to the scene, flying in medicines, food, water, blankets and tents, and bringing out 1,100 injured survivors for treatment in Mashad and Teheran.

Left: Over the years, C-130s have been involved in many international relief operations; carrying Bangladeshi refugee families. *Lockheed*

Below: An RAF Hercules C1 at Van airport, Turkey, after bringing in relief supplies for the victims of the November 1976 earthquake in the area. *MoD*

Above left: An RAF C1 manoeuvres its way gingerly down a remote valley in Nepal in the Himalayas after air-dropping food to villagers during the 1977 famine-relief operation. *Lockheed*

Left: RAF men load relief supplies in Nepal ready for placing on board one of the four C1s which took part in the relief operation. The food was sent by Canada, the United States, and the World Food Programme, and was either dropped without parachute from 50ft, or with parachutes from 600ft. *Lockheed*

Right: Natives help unload food from a British RAF Hercules in the drought and famine-hit West African Republic of Mali. *MoD*

Darwin, Australia 1974: the city was devastated by cyclone Tracy, and the first aircraft to reach the scene was the C-130 of the Royal Australian Air Force, landing by the light of paraffin flares. RAAF Hercules flew non-stop for days and nights, ferrying in supplies, and bringing out the injured. On one evacuation run, with 180 passengers on board, a Hercules was struck by lightning in a bad storm, but flew on. The RAAF captain said after landing: 'The Hercules is a very forgiving aeroplane . . . If it were any other type of aircraft, I don't know what would have happened.'

Zaire, 1976: A Royal Canadian Air Force Hercules rushed a medical isolation unit into the country after its northern quarter had been struck by the green monkey virus, a highly-infectious killer disease, which brought about 300 deaths within the space of two weeks. The Zaire Air Force also had C-130s in its fleet, and utilised them to bring in much-needed medical supplies to fight the epidemic.

Saudi Arabia, 1977: when four people were seriously injured in a car accident in a remote area 125 miles away from the nearest hospital in Riyadh, a Hercules of the Royal Saudi Air Force flew to the scene, landed on the road, picked them up, then took off from the road and ferried them to the city for treatment.

Tripura, India, 1971: USAF Hercules were involved in the aftermath of the refugee evacuation from East Pakistan, mentioned earlier. They moved the homeless arriving at Tripura, in the east of India, to safer areas in Assam, and then carried back a million units of cholera vaccine and 20 tons of rice a day to feed the thousands who remained. As many as 190 refugees were carried on flights out, and some were so relieved to be given a place on board that they insisted on climbing into the flight deck and kissing the feet of the aviators.

The sub-Sahara area of Africa, 1973, and onwards: the United Nations Food and Agriculture Organisa-tion co-ordinated a world-wide drive for grain and air transport to meet the drought that swept across the area, and six nations, Switzerland, the US, Sweden, Belgium, Britain and Canada, sent Hercules to carry the food, in an encouraging example of international relief. The aircraft flew into remote airstrips with supplies, and particularly powdered milk, for the nomads of the vast area affected by the drought, which had lasted seven years at that time. In doing so, the aircraft braved natural hazards, including bird strikes and sandstorms.

The impression remains that many of the countries which have bought Hercules for their air forces have had 'country-building' tasks also very firmly in mind for the aircraft. Thailand, for instance, bought three advanced C-130Hs in 1980, and utilised them not only for military logistics, but to serve remote communities in the mountainous areas in the north and east, and in the dense jungles of the south.

The first of six C-130Hs ordered by the Government of Algeria, and operated by the Algerian Air Force, was used in a rescue which hit world headlines — finding Mark Thatcher, the son of the British Prime Minister, after he had become lost in the desert on a motor car rally. Manned by a joint crew from the Algerian Air Force and Lockheed, the Hercules spotted Thatcher in the Sahara and then, utilising its inertial navigation system (INS), which gives a constant 'present position' read-out, noted the latitude and longitude, before calling in a ground rescue team. The incident took place in January 1982.

The Government of the Philippines bought four civil L-100-20 versions of the Hercules to 'tie together' that nation's 7,100 islands. The aircraft are used for a multitude of tasks, carrying, for instance, bulldozers and other road-building equipment to remote spots, and when not used for shifting cargo, being pressed into service for weather research, typhoon reconnaissance photogrammetry, and earth-resources measurements

Right: One of the largest fleets of L-100-30s was bought by Indonesia. Its seven civilian Herks have been used largely to further its transmigration policy, under which entire families are transported by air from over-populated regions in Java and Bali to agricultural homesteads on outlying islands. *Lockheed*

Below right: Pelita Air Service civil Hercules took part in the Indonesian transmigration operation. *Lockheed*

The Philippines Government has also earmarked the Hercules for emergency tasks, such as speeding food, clothing and shelter to the victims of natural disasters, tasks which C-130s called in from the United States have performed in the past.

The Government of Peru also ordered L-100-20s and pressed them into duty on a wide variety of commercial transport work, including the airlifting of purebred cattle, fish, and military supplies. The Hercules also carried heavy equipment over the Andes for the development of Peruvian oilfields near the headwaters of the Amazon river.

Indonesia took L-100-30s on to its inventory largely to further its transmigration programme, under which entire families were transported by air from over-populated regions of Java and Bali to fertile new agricultural homesteads on outlying islands. Indonesia is the fifth-largest nation in the world in terms of population, and the goal for its transmigration airlift is 12,000 families, or 60,000 people, each month, a goal which could have never even been approached without the Hercules. Each of the Hercules on the Indonesian flights takes 128 people and their entire personal belongings.

Hercules serving with the Bolivian Air Force lifting more than half a million pounds of heavy construction equipment over the Andes, four-miles high, from La Paz to the Amazon basin, during an airlift lasting 17 days. The equipment was needed to build a sugar cane mill, and the heavily-laden aircraft touched down without trouble on a grass strip only 4,000ft long. Individual loads included earth-movers weighing 14 tons apiece. The Hercules had to climb to 23,000ft to clear the Andes mountain range, and then drop down to the landing strip whose altitude was only 900ft, but despite the rugged conditions, the entire airlift went without any operational delay, and with no downtime necessary for maintenance.

The tiny nation of Gabon, on the west coast of Africa, with a population of half a million, uses its Hercules to airlift all types of loads into its dense jungle interior. The cargo has included an entire supermarket, picked up at the capital, Libreville, and flown to a provincial community.

Peru used the Herks to open up its remote inland towns on the Amazon plateau with road connections to the Pacific coast. The aircraft flew in heavy road construction equipment, shifting over 500 tons of tractors, bulldozers and graders over the Andes in 38 missions. First arrivals of Hercules in the Peruvian villages could produce exciting moments for their crews. At an airstrip outside the small community of Mendoza, where two 15,000lb bulldozers, a compressor, and 20 engineers were delivered, the aircraft was surrounded by a chanting, shouting throng of villagers who, singing their national anthem, picked up the pilots, hoisted them on their shoulders and then paraded them around. For the villagers, the arrival of

Above: Three different versions of the Hercules are operated by Gabon's Forces Aeriennes Gabonaises, a C-130H, an L-100-20, and two L-100-30s. The aircraft are used mainly to transport heavy equipment to remote sites up-country. *Lockheed*

Below: The Peruvian Air Force, the Fuerza Aerea del Peru, is unusual in that its Hercules are of the civilian type, L-100-20s, of which it has eight in the inventory. The inventory also includes the Herk's rival from the Eastern bloc, the Antonov 26. *Lockheed*

the Herk and its road-making equipment meant the prospect of a link with the outside world, and a market for their products — tea and coffee, sugar cane, tobacco, cotton and cattle.

Peruvian Hercules also supported the construction of an oil pipeline over the Andes — and helped to reduce the price of fish in a remote section of that country. Fish had traditionally been carried from Lima to the inland town of Aycucho by trucks, each hauling a four-ton load, and taking 22 hours to drive through the precipitous mountains. The Herks lifted 20 tons at a time over the mountains in one hour — and did the job far more cheaply.

Morocco uses its Hercules to transport fresh fruit and vegetables, and other products to centres in Europe, and the aircraft then pick up cargoes to take home. Outward bound, for instance, the aircraft have each carried 20,000lb of Moroccan-made clothing, and a ton of frozen fish; inward, the load has been 140,000 baby chicks loaded at Amsterdam.

Abu Dhabi used its Hercules to import 4,000 rare date palms from Tunisia. The load was valued at more than $1million, but was a gift from one Arab nation to another. Two C-130s took part in the lift, each loaded with 2,000 trees, each of which stood 4ft high and weighed 20lb. To keep the delicate plants alive during their transition, their roots were packed in wooden boxes, and their fronds were sprayed just before take-off to keep the moisture level up. On the arrival of the Hercules, the trees were quickly taken off and moved into a plant nursery where a special sand had been prepared and fertilised. After acclimatisation, the trees were planted along roads in Abu Dhabi, and within a year were bearing fruit.

It is fitting to conclude this chapter on the Hercules as an 'angel of mercy' with the story of Commander John F. Paulus, one of the most experienced of the United States Navy's ski-Hercules pilots. Paulus retired from the USN in late 1981 after a lengthy career which included nine seasons of flying into the Antarctic, and with 4,500 flight hours on the LC-130. When he made his 285th and final landing at McMurdo Sound, the Navy's South Pole ice station, he was told that the landing field had been renamed in his honour.

During his career with the USN's Antarctic support squadron, Cdr Paulus was in charge of a number of notable flights. He piloted the first LC-130 to land to establish Siple Station, 2,250nm from McMurdo, and that same season, 1970, saw him fly the first group of women scientists to the South Pole. In two medical missions to Russian scientific stations, he evacuated a dying Soviet scientist, and dropped oxygen bottles for a critically-ill Japanese.

In August 1974, he flew an LC-130 from Antarctica to New Zealand with one of the aircraft's four propellers feathered. The 'plane lost the engine when taking-off from McMurdo, and Paulus made the decision to continue, on the grounds that there was no maintenance crew on the ice. The aircraft flew over water, carrying 12 crew and 16 passengers, for nine hours on three engines, but despite the loss of power, it performed beautifully. The USN's 'ski-birds' flock to Antarctica every year in October, the beginning of spring there, to resupply stations as they emerge from the long winter. The LC-130 is the world's largest ski-equipped transport aircraft. Its skis, the two largest of which weigh a ton apiece, are coated with Teflon to resist snow. The LC-130 also retains its wheeled undercarriage, enabling its crews to operate off of either paved surfaces, or ice and snow.

Below: Side-on view shows clearly the ski/wheel arrangement of the US Navy's ski-fitted Hercules. These were originally designated UB-1L, then C-130BL, then LC-130F. *Lockheed*

10
Hercules into the Future

The Hercules made its maiden flight in August 1954, and at the time of writing, nearly 30 years later, is still being produced by Lockheed at its Marietta, Georgia, plant at the rate of three each month, with new orders still coming in. The Herk has been kept 'young' by its simple basic design which has defied aviation fads and fancies down the decades, by its ruggedness and STOL capabilities, by its dozens of different uses, and by its miserly fuel consumption in an age of high kerosene prices, with the threat that they will go even higher in the future.

For Lockheed, the ungainly-looking 'bird' has been a winner. Its Hercules programme has generated well over $6billion gross sales in new aircraft and spares, $4billion of that total in new aircraft alone. Written off by its critics in the 1950s as a mistake with only a short production life ahead of it, the type has run and run, being constantly improved through the C-130A, the C-130B, the E and the H models, and most recently the 'advanced H', known inevitably as the Super. The industrial team which has helped to polish the aircraft as the years have gone by include some of the best-known names in aerospace on either side of the Atlantic — Avco, Detriot Diesel Allison, Collins Air Transport, Hamilton Standard, Litton Aero Products, Marshall of Cambridge, Menasco, Rohr Industries, the Scottish division of British Aerospace, Texas Instruments, Rolls-Royce and Vought.

Improvements in the structure and systems of the basic design of the early 1950s have offered better payload, speed, range, service life and take-off distance to operators, most of whom have placed repeat orders, while over half have come back three, four and even five times. Lockheed's boast is that the C-130 programme has been ahead of schedule and under budget from the beginning, and that almost 100% of the 1,700-plus aircraft which have now rolled off the Marietta line have been delivered either ahead of, or on contract dates. Lockheed directors, in the mid-1950s,

would, it is said, have been happy to see a production run of 300 machines.

Amazingly, the Hercules today still looks externally much the same as it did around 30 years ago, low-slung, its belly only 45in of the ground. As mentioned above, the improvements have almost all been inside. The A model was designed to have a gross weight of 108,000lb and a payload of 25,000lb, and its four Allison turboprops to generate a total of 14,200eshp. Speed was to be 360mph, and take-off distance over a 50ft obstacle at 120,000lb gross 3,650ft. Maximum range called for was 3,000 miles. With the B model, speed was increased to 375mph, gross weight to 135,000lb, more-powerful engines produced a total of 16,200eshp, and the four-bladed Hamilton-Standard propeller, replacing three-bladed Curtiss-Wright props, gave quieter operations. Maximum range went up to 4,000 miles.

Then came the E model, produced originally for MATS — now Military Airlift Command — of the USAF, and this increased the cargo-carrying capability of the Hercules to 45,328lb, with a rise in gross weight to 155,000lb. With the 'E', C-130 operators could cross the Atlantic non-stop, and the Pacific with one stop, while carrying 27,000lb. Pylon fuel tanks appeared under the wings. The H version raised the range still further — 5,470 miles while being ferried, 4,750 miles with a 20,000lb payload, 2,350 miles carrying maximum payload of 45,000lb. Further improvements in the Allison T56-A-15 turboprops brought the total power up to 19,640eshp. Stretches of 8ft, and then 15ft on the original C-130 fuselage produced two versions for the civil market, the dash 20 and the dash 30.

Lockheed refers to this steady progression as, 'developing a new aircraft in a proven framework', and following this principle, the company has, during the three decades since the Hercules first appeared, increased its payload by 22%, its speed by 11%, its range by 52%, and shortened the take-off distance by 17%. Carroll Dallas, chief design engineer at Lockheed-Georgia, says he feels that the most important improvements that have been introduced have been those to the wing.

During the late 1960s, the company's designers analysed the intensive stress to which the C-130s had been subjected in its rough-field assignments in Vietnam. As a result, they produced an improved centre wing box aimed at giving it better ability to withstand such tasks, but also to extend the aircraft's life. A new centre wing structure was tested in a fatigue rig to 40,000 simulated flight hours, and the results were so encouraging that Lockheed retrofitted not only ex-Vietnam Herks, but those of all other operators — with the exception of the original A models.

A total of 594 C-130s returned to Marietta to have the 'long-life' centre box grafted on, including aircraft from Australia, New Zealand, Brazil, Iran, Pakistan, Saudi Arabia, Indonesia and Colombia, and in early 1969 the Marietta assembly line began incorporating the improvement into new aircraft. Three years later, Lockheed engineers made structural design improvements on the C-130's outer wings to give them the same fatigue standards as the new centre box, and this change was incorporated into the production line in 1973.

The aluminium alloy of which the overall wing structure is made has been upgraded to a new stress corrosion resistant standard 7075-T73, with a sulphuric acid-anodised surface as a base for polyurethane protective coating. The wing-box structures are now also fay-surface sealed on assembly with a Lockheed-developed corrosion-inhibitive polysulfide sealant, while structural fasteners are wet-installed with like material, and external joints and seams are further protected with an environmental aerodynamic-smoother sealant. Integral fuel tanks in the wings formed by this sealed structure are made even tighter by fillet-sealing and fastener-overcoating techniques. To eliminate bacteria forming in water remaining in the bottom of the tanks, the new wings are equipped with a suction system, actuated by the fuel-boost pumps — a system which was pioneered on the C-5A Galaxy freighter.

The Herk's contemporary avionics package also reflects the march of technology through its three decades of development. Wheras the first model had a single, early-vintage gyro compass, those coming off the assembly line today are fitted with two Sperry C-12s of an advanced type. Solid-state avionics have replaced vacuum tubes, and integrated circuits have taken over from discrete components. Current avionics systems available include AN/APN 59E(V)

Right: Southern Air L-100-20 take-off shows the extent of the interim stretch of the civil Hercules, carried out in 1967, which added 8ft 4in to the fuselage length over the basic C-130, and offered considerably better operating economics to non-military operators. *Lockheed*

Below: The L-100-30C, a passenger and cargo convertible, is just one of the futuristic versions of the Hercules which Lockheed's design teams have been working on over the years in an effort to squeeze the last drops out of the company's highly-successful original design. Others have included bigger versions, a twin-engined version, the L-400, and there was even a proposal at one stage for an amphibian, with a glass-fibre hull fitted over the wheels.

search and weather radar, dual 5LRV-4 AN/ APN-127 VOR/ILS/MB navigation receivers, the AN/APN-171 radio altimeter, FD 109 flight director, AP 105 automatic pilot, AN/ARN-118 TACAN, DF 206 ADF, AN/ARC 104 UHF, the AN/ARC 186 VHF, the AN/APN-169A intraformation positioning set, the AN/APN-147 doppler navigator, the ASN-35A navigational computer, and the AN/ARN 131 Omega.

From 1975 onwards, new C-130s coming off the Marietta line had a new airliner-type auxiliary power unit, the GTCP 85-18OC, built by AiResearch. This gave the Hercules crews the ability for the first time to operate the APU in flight to supply additional electrical power for the aircraft. The new APU, located in the landing gear pod, replaced the gas-turbine generator and the air turbine motor. Aileron, rudder and elevator actuators have been improved through the incorporation of newer fatigue-resistant material, and longer-life seals. All of the fasteners in rotating joints of the flight-control system have been changed from plain castellated nuts with cotter pins, to self-locking castellated nuts with cotter pins. In some more critical locations of fasteners, self-retaining bolts have been introduced. In the engine-control cable system, larger-diameter pulleys, and longer-life 7 by 19 stainless-steel cable has been introduced to increase the life of the cables.

Other upgradings have been made over the years to the Hercules' hydraulics and air-conditioning systems and, partly as a result of lessons learned in Vietnam, to the landing gear. Latest versions of the aircraft have higher-capacity multi-disc brakes with modulating, individual wheel control anti-skid systems giving decreased brake fade. Wheels are now made of forged aluminium for better fatigue resistance, and to prevent tyre blow-outs from overheated brakes, fusible plugs are used on the main wheels.

Dallas says, proudly: 'What we have done is to build on what was a great basic design to give the Herk increased reliability and maintainability and increased performance, while bringing our production learning curve and costs down to the point at which the C-130 is the best bargain to be found in an airlifter. I have had a chance to see just how a great 'plane can become even greater, and reach for its potential through state-of-the-art improvements brought about by a continuous production run, such as our Hercules has enjoyed. We have now built so many different models and versions of the Herk', he adds with a smile, 'that when we get an inquiry about it, we have to ask, "Just which Hercules are you talking about".'

And Lockheed is still planning to improve its venerable workhorse design further. During 1982, with Detriot Diesel Allison and the USAF's Aeronautical Systems Division, it tested a more-powerful 5,000hp derivative engine, designated the XT56-A-100, which, if fitted to C-130s, would save the air force, which bought over 1,000 Hercules alone, over $40million a year in reduced fuel consumption. In tests carried out at Wright Patterson AFB, Ohio, the new version of the engine produced a power increase of 23% over T56-A-15, and burned between 9 and 14% less fuel.

Lockheed claimed that if fitted to the MAC fleet, it would produce additional savings of $3.5million for improved reliability and maintainability, equivalent to having a half a squadron more aircraft available for MAC missions. The XT56-A-100 would show a range increase of 8%, a 500ft/min increase in rate of climb, a 4,000ft higher cruise altitude, an increase of 25kts speed for air-to-air refuelling, and a 36% hot day payload increase.

Obviously there is still a lot of life left in the Herk yet, and it is clear that this propeller-powered workhorse which has survived into and through the era of the pure-jet transport will still be hauling the troops and their equipment, bringing succour in flood, famine and other natural and man-made disasters, and carrying out its hundred-and-one other tasks, well into the 21st century.

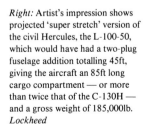

Right: Artist's impression shows projected 'super stretch' version of the civil Hercules, the L-100-50, which would have had a two-plug fuselage addition totalling 45ft, giving the aircraft an 85ft long cargo compartment — or more than twice that of the C-130H — and a gross weight of 185,000lb. *Lockheed*

Appendices

1 Hercules Orders/Deliveries by Customer

	Total	C-130A	C-130B	C-130E	C-130H	C-130H-30	L-100	L-100-20	L-100-30
US Government	1,073/1,047	219/219	209/209	402/402	243/217				
Commercial/ Export	624/604	12/12	21/21	86/86	397/385	12/9	21/21	28/28	47/42
Total:	1,697/1,651*	231/231	230/230	488/488	640/602	12/9	21/21	28/28	47/42

*All figures correct up to the end of third quarter 1982. Total exceeded 1,700 early 1983.

Domestic	Total	C-130A	C-130B	C-130E	C-130H	C-130H-30	L-100	L-100-20	L-100-30
US Government									
Air Force*	902/902	219/219	140/140	397/397	146/146				
Air Reserve Forces	38/23				38/23				
Coast Guard	30/25		12/12	1/1	17/12				
Marine Corps	64/60		46/46		18/14				
Navy	17/17		11/11		6/6				
TACAMO	22/20			4/4	18/16				
US (Civil)									
Air America	1/1							1/1	
Airlift Int'l	4/4						4/4		
Alaska Airlines	3/3						3/3		
Alaska Int'l Air	3/3								3/3
Delta Air Lines	3/3						3/3		
Flying W	2/2							2/2	
Interior Airways	1/1							1/1	
Nat'l A/C Lsg	3/3						3/3		
PLS Air Lease	1/1							1/1	
So Air Trans	2/2							2/2	
Transamerica	7/7							3/3	4/4

*Includes 16 MAP Aircraft

Note: Hercules Transports included among the original deliveries listed in the foregoing table were subsequently acquired as shown below:

Domestic	Total	C-130A	C-130B	C-130E	C-130H	C-130H-30	L-100	L-100-20	L-100-30
Alaska Int'l Air	3								3
Angola — TAAG	1							1	
Colombia	3		3						
Echo Bay Mines	1							1	
Jordan	2		2						
Pacific Western	1							1	
Pakistan	11		10	1					
Philippine Aero	2							2	
Singapore	4		4						
So Air Trans	1								1
Transamerica	5								5
Turkey	8			8					
Uganda Airlines	1								1
United African A/L	1							1	
United Trade Int'l	1								1
US NASA	1		1						

Left: Justified jubilation at Lockheed-Georgia as the 1,600th Hercules, a C-130H-30 for Indonesia, is rolled out. Left to right; Woody Mayfield, Lockheed flight-line director, Robert Roche, Lockheed VP Hercules programmes, and Leo Sullivan, Lockheed assistant chief design engineer. Sales of Herks worldwide have since topped the 1,700, and look like going on for a long time yet.

International	Total	C-130A	C-130B	C-130E	C-130H	C-130H-30	L-100	L-100-20	L-100-30
Abu Dhabi	4/4				4/4				
Algeria	14/6				10/4	4/2			
Air Algerie	3/3								3/3
Angola TAAG	2/2							2/2	
Argentina	11/10				10/10				1/0
Australia	36/36	12/12		12/12	12/12				
Belgium	12/12				12/12				
Bolivia	3/3				2/2				1/1
Brazil	16/16			11/11	5/5				
Cameroon	3/2				2/2	1/0			
Canada Armed Forces	33/33		4/4	24/24	5/5				
Maple Leaf Lsg	1/1							1/1	
Pacific Western	3/3						1/1	1/1	1/1
Chile	2/2				2/2				
Colombia	See Note								
Denmark	3/3				3/3				
Dubai	1/1								1/1
Ecuador	3/3				3/3				
Egypt	23/20				23/20				
Gabon	4/4				1/1			1/1	2/2
Greece	12/12				12/12				
Indonesia	28/28		10/10		4/4	7/7			7/7
Iran	60/60			28/28	32/32				
Israel	12/12				12/12				
Italy	14/14				14/14				
Japan	2/0				2/0				
Jordan	4/4				4/4				
Kuwait	6/2							2/2	4/0
Libya	16/16				16/16				
Malaysia	9/9				9/9				
Mexico	1/1								1/1
Morocco	19/19				19/19				
New Zealand	5/5				5/5				
Niger	2/2				2/2				
Nigeria	6/6				6/6				
Norway	6/6				6/6				
Oman	3/2				3/2				
Pakistan (Gov't)	See Note								
Pakistan Int'l Air	2/2						2/2		
Peru	8/8							8/8	
Philippines	5/5				3/3			2/2	
Portugal	5/5				5/5				
Saudi Arabia	45/45			9/9	36/36				
Singapore	4/4				4/4				
South Africa (Gov't)	7/7		7/7						
Safair	17/17								17/17
Safmarine	1/1							1/1	
Spain	12/12				12/12				
Sudan	6/6				6/6				
Sweden	8/8			2/2	6/6				
Thailand	3/3				3/3				
Turkey	See Note								
United Kingdom	66/66				66/66				
Venezuela	7/7				7/7				
W Germany Wirtschaftsflug	1/1								1/1
Yemen (North)	2/2				2/2				
Zaire (Gov't)	7/7				7/7				
SCIBE	1/1								1/1
Zambia (Gov't)	3/3						3/3		
Zambian Air Cargo	2/2						2/2		

2 C-130H/C-130H-30

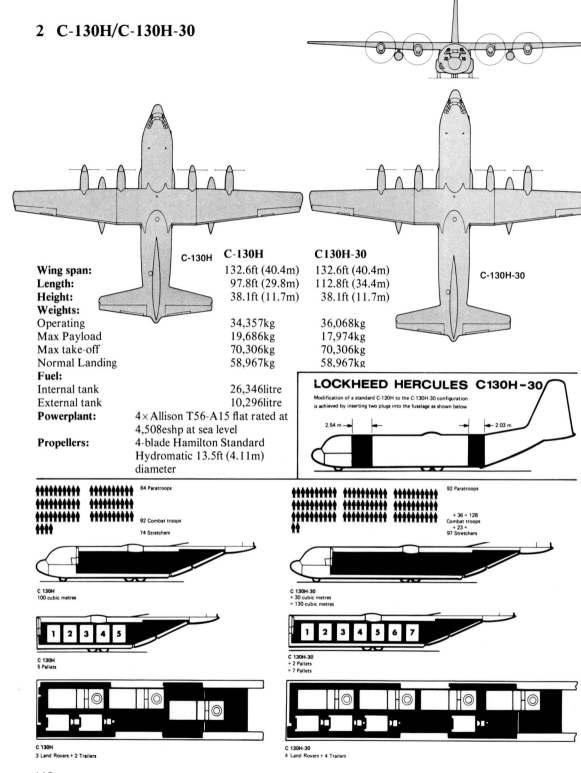

	C-130H	C130H-30
Wing span:	132.6ft (40.4m)	132.6ft (40.4m)
Length:	97.8ft (29.8m)	112.8ft (34.4m)
Height:	38.1ft (11.7m)	38.1ft (11.7m)
Weights:		
Operating	34,357kg	36,068kg
Max Payload	19,686kg	17,974kg
Max take-off	70,306kg	70,306kg
Normal Landing	58,967kg	58,967kg
Fuel:		
Internal tank	26,346litre	
External tank	10,296litre	
Powerplant:	4×Allison T56-A15 flat rated at 4,508eshp at sea level	
Propellers:	4-blade Hamilton Standard Hydromatic 13.5ft (4.11m) diameter	

LOCKHEED HERCULES C130H-30

Modification of a standard C-130H to the C-130H-30 configuration is achieved by inserting two plugs into the fuselage as shown below

2.54 m   2.03 m

64 Paratroops
92 Combat troops
74 Stretchers

92 Paratroops
+ 36 = 128 Combat troops
+ 23 = 97 Stretchers

C 130H
100 cubic metres

C 130H-30
+ 30 cubic metres
= 130 cubic metres

C 130H
5 Pallets

1 2 3 4 5

C 130H-30
+ 2 Pallets
= 7 Pallets

1 2 3 4 5 6 7

C 130H
3 Land Rovers + 2 Trailers

C 130H-30
4 Land Rovers + 4 Trailers

110

3 L-100-30 Super Hercules

Weights
Max ramp weight: 155,800lb (70,670kg)
Max take-off gross weight: 155,000lb (70,307kg)
Max landing weight: 135,000lb (61,235kg)
Zero fuel weight: 127,000lb (57,606kg)
Operating weight empty*: 73,413lb (33,300kg)
Max payload: 53,587lb (24,306kg)
Usable fuel: 6,955gal (26,327lit)
   At 6.7lb/USgal: 46,602lb (21,139kg)

*Specification weight less external tanks. (Does not
include cargo handling equipment.)

Cargo compartment dimensions
Length: 55ft 5in (16.89m)
Width: 10ft (3.05m)

Height: 9ft (2.74m)
Bulk volume: 6,057sq ft (172cu m)

Powerplant
4 Allison 501-D22A turboprops with Hamilton
   Standard four blade propellers, 13ft 6in (4.11m)
   diameter
Take-off power: 4,508eshp (3,362kw)

Performance
Take-off field length: 6,000ft (1,829m)
Landing field length: 4,850ft (1,478m)
Range (230sm+45min fuel reserve):
   Max payload: 1,428sm (2,298km)
   Max fuel: 3,033sm (4,882km)
   Ferry: 4,170sm (6,712km)
Max cruise speed: 362mph (583km/hr)
Max certificated ceiling: 32,600ft (9,936m)

Maximum payload missions

Distance	200sm	500sm	1,000sm
Field length (ft/m)	4,880/1,463*	4,800/1,487	5,480/1,670
Flight time (hr+min):	0+41	1+35	3+03
Flight fuel (lb/kg):	3,646/1,654	7,501/3,402	14,535/6,593

*Landing field length limited.

4 HC-130H Characteristics

Dimensions
Length (yoke retracted): 100.5ft
Height: 38.3ft
Wing span: 132.6ft
Main fuselage compartment length (excluding ramp):
   41.4ft
Ramp length: 10.3ft
Engines
Manufacturer: Allison
Type: Prop-jet
Number and model: (4) T56-A-14
Take-off rating: 4,910eshp*
Normal rating: 4,365eshp
Propellers
Manufacturer: Hamilton Standard
Model: 54H60-91
Diameter: 13.5ft
Number of blades: 4
Weights
Design max take-off (2.5g load factor): 155,000lb
Contingency max take-off (2.25g load factor):
   175,000lb
Max landing
   5ft/sec Sink Rate: 175,000lb
   9ft/sec Sink Rate: 130,000lb
Equipped weight empty: 85,000 to 87,000lb

Crew
Basic: 10 men
Augmented: 13 men
Fuel Capacity

	USgal	Pounds JP-4
Total without fuselage tanks:	9,680	62,920
Two fuselage tanks (removable):	3,600	23,400
Total:	13,280	86,320†

Loading opening
Height (ODS installed): 7.5ft
Height (ODS removed): 9.0ft
Width: 10.0ft
Height above ground: 3.4ft
Airport Performance (sea level, std day, normal operation)
Take-off (155,000lb)
   Ground roll: 3,520ft
   Distance over 50ft: 4,250ft
Landing (130,000lb)
   Ground roll: 2,180ft‡
   Distance from 50ft: 3,750ft‡

---

*Flat rated to 19,600 in/lbs of torque (4,200shp).
†Take-off weight is normally limited to 155,000lb; the
  maximum fuel load is therefore limited to between
  73,601lb and 66,275lb, depending upon the actual
  equipped weight empty.
‡Using 4-engine reverse thrust.

Rate of Climb (sea level, std day, normal rated power)

Gross weight (lb)	Climb rate (ft/min)
115,000	2,860
155,000	1,850
175,000	1,490

Cruise speeds
Long-range cruise (Avg): 299kt
Maximum cruise speed: 344kt

5 KC-130R Tanker/Transport Characteristics

Weights
Max take-off
  Tanker: 155,000lb
  Cargo transport (2.5g): 155,000lb
Operating weight
  Tanker: 85,277lb
  Cargo transport: 78,671lb
Payload
  Refuelling fuel — zero radius: 69,723lb
  Cargo (2.5g): 40,471lb
Fuel capacity
  Cargo transport (9,680gal): 62,920lb
  Tanker (13,280gal): 86,320lb

Performance
Aerial refuelling fuel at 1,000nm: 30,800lb
Range (25,000lb payload): 3,050nm
Take-off distance (155,000lb): 5,200ft
Landing distance (130,000lb): 2,470ft
Average cruise speed — cargo mission: 280KtAS
Aerial refuelling speed at 20,000ft: 315KtAS
Refuelling system
Fuel pressure: 120lb/sq in
Fuel flow rate — each drogue: 300gal/min
Distance between drogues: 91ft
Pod diameter: 45in
Hose diameter: 2.375in

Below: KC-130 tankers of the US Marines, one of which is seen here refuelling two USMC F-18 Hornets, have a flight crew of five plus two refuelling observers. They can be converted to the transport role. *Lockheed*